Fed by
God's Grace

Fed by God's Grace

COMMUNION PRAYERS for

Year C

Michael E. Dixon
Sandy Dixon

Chalice Press®

St. Louis, Missouri

Cover design: Elizabeth Wright
Cover art: Detail from window by Francis Deck at St. Agnes Church,
    Springfield, Ill. Photo © The Crosiers
Interior design: Elizabeth Wright

This book is printed on acid-free, recycled paper.

Visit Chalice Press on the World Wide Web at
www.chalicepress.com

10 9 8 7 6 5 4 3 2 1   00 01 02 03 04 05

Library of Congress Cataloging–in–Publication Data

Dixon, Michael E.
    Fed by God's grace : Communion prayers for Year C / by Michael
E. Dixon and Sandy Dixon.
        p.   cm.
    ISBN 0-8272-1028-0
    1. Eucharistic prayers.   2. Common lectionary (1992). I. Dixon,
Sandy.   II. Title.
BV825.54 .D59 2000
264'.13 — dc21   00-010057
                                                                    CIP

Printed in the United States of America

Contents

Introduction

The table is ready. Worshipers gather. We sing, we pray, we hear the Word. We are invited to come to the table, to eat and drink, to do as Christ's disciples did in the upper room long ago. And we pray. The spoken prayers of the leaders mingle with the unspoken prayers of the community. Then, by the grace of God, we are spiritually fed.

Fed by God's Grace, Communion Prayers for Year C is one of three books designed for those of you who are called on to pray aloud at Christ's table. We hope that these prayers will serve as promptings, models, or clues to give you input as you prepare your own prayers. If they stimulate your thoughts, sharpen your insights, and focus your attention, they will serve their purposes. If, on some Sundays, you want to use the prayers as written here, adopting these words as your own, that's all right too.

Many previous books of communion prayers have followed a single model, such as separate prayers for the bread and the cup. *Fed by God's Grace* offers more models. For each Sunday, you will find four prayers: one for the bread, one for the cup, a unified prayer for both bread and cup, and a closing prayer to be used after the communion service. That way you can choose the model that is best for your congregation.

We offer these suggestions on how to prepare for praying at the Lord's table.

- If your congregation uses the Revised Common Lectionary, check to see what Sunday of the church year you will be praying, then find the appropriate page in this book.

- If your congregation does not use the Revised Common Lectionary, it may follow the general seasons of the church year. Find a set of prayers appropriate to the season.
- If your congregation does not use the Revised Common Lectionary and you want to choose a prayer that connects with the scripture lesson for the day, use the scripture index in the back of the book.
- When you have selected a prayer, read and reflect on all the scripture readings at the top of the page. This is a part of your spiritual preparation for serving at the table and can help you understand the concepts behind the prayer.
- Read the prayer to yourself (and to God) as spiritual preparation and rehearsal. Revise the prayer as necessary to fit your own beliefs or those of your congregation or denomination, and to fit any particular contexts of your local situation. Write out the prayer, make notes, or commit it to memory, as is right for you.
- Before the service begins, spend a few moments in silent prayer and reflection or take time to pray together with others who are leading worship.

As mentioned above, these collections of prayers for the communion table follow the seasons of the church year, which begins in late November or early December with Advent, the season of preparation before Christmas. From there we move into Epiphany, Lent, Eastertide, and finally Pentecost, the longest season of the church year. The Revised Common Lectionary, a three-year cycle of scripture readings increasingly being used in many congregations, follows a progression of scripture passages designed to give the minister and congregation an overview of the Bible: Hebrew Scriptures, psalms, epistles, and gospels. For year A, the major gospel is Matthew, year B Mark, and year C Luke. All three years use John.

Prayers in *Fed by God's Grace* pick their eucharistic themes from the lectionary scriptures. Not every scripture is used in each Sunday's set of prayers, but we tried to touch base with the themes, if not the words, of each set of scripture texts.

We have used as our source of scripture listings *The Revised Common Lectionary,* developed by the Consultation on Common Texts and published in 1992. Following the lectionary plan, this book has built in all the variables for the calendar years. Confusingly, not all the seasons are the same length from year to year. Lent counts forty days backward from the date of Easter, and Pentecost falls seven Sundays after Easter. Since Easter moves, Epiphany may be very short and Pentecost very long in a given year, or Epiphany will be longer and Pentecost shorter in another year. You might want to check with the pastor to see what Sunday of the church year you will be serving at the table.

We offer the following chart so that you will know when to use these books:

Year A
Advent 2001: last Sunday of Pentecost 2002
Advent 2004: last Sunday of Pentecost 2005
Advent 2007: last Sunday of Pentecost 2008
Advent 2010: last Sunday of Pentecost 2011

Year B
Advent 2002: last Sunday of Pentecost 2003
Advent 2005: last Sunday of Pentecost 2006
Advent 2008: last Sunday of Pentecost 2009
Advent 2011: last Sunday of Pentecost 2012

Year C
Advent 2000: last Sunday of Pentecost 2001
Advent 2003: last Sunday of Pentecost 2004
Advent 2006: last Sunday of Pentecost 2007
Advent 2009: last Sunday of Pentecost 2010

First Sunday of Advent

Jeremiah 33:14–16
Psalm 25:1–10
1 Thessalonians 3:9–13
Luke 21:25–36

PRAYER FOR THE BREAD: To you, O God, we lift up our souls. In you we put our trust. You are a merciful God, and your steadfast love leads us on the paths of faithfulness. We see your mercy at this table, as we break the bread, for we are fed by your grace. We remember your love at this table, because the bread recalls for us the Christ that you sent to save us. May your Spirit prepare our hearts for our Savior that we might learn to love as we have been loved, to be merciful as we have received mercy. Amen.

PRAYER FOR THE CUP: Good and gracious God, we continue in prayer at this, your table. Long ago, you gave a promise to your people that you would send a righteous and just leader to bring salvation. We believe that Jesus Christ came to fulfill that promise. The cup we drink reminds us of why Jesus came into our midst, to offer his life so we might know real life with you. As we begin this Advent season, we pray that your Spirit will prepare our hearts and minds to accept Christ's ways as ours in a deeper way than we have done before. Amen.

UNIFIED PRAYER: Renew us, O God, as we come to your table. We are a take-charge people who are uncomfortable trusting in a future that only you can control. We are a here-and-now people who have difficulty in preparation and planning, even when the one we are preparing for is your Son and our Savior, Jesus the Christ. Even when we can get our heads and hearts around preparing for the coming of the baby in Bethlehem, we are awkward and uncomfortable in thinking about Christ returning in glory. Teach us here at your table, dear God, that we may learn to trust you completely with our lives, and that we may turn our will over to be guided by yours. For it is here at this table that we learn how Jesus Christ, in complete trust and love, offered himself for us. Through this bread we eat and this cup we drink, let us offer ourselves to your loving and gracious will. May your Spirit work within our hearts as we partake. Amen.*

PRAYER AFTER COMMUNION: God of love and mercy, we thank you for this time of communion, and pray that through it we may increase and abound in love for one another and for all, just as we abound in love for you. Amen.

*Sandy Dixon, *Everlasting Light* (St. Louis: Chalice Press, 2000), pp. 52–53.

Second Sunday of Advent

Malachi 3:1–4
Luke 1:68–79
Philippians 1:3–11
Luke 3:1–6

PRAYER FOR THE BREAD: Plant within us the seeds of righteousness, nurturing God. Sustain their growth and increase their harvest, abundant God. Purify and cleanse us, O renewing God. As Christ offered himself up as bread for the world, may we offer ourselves in loving service. May this bread that we now break nourish our bodies and spirits to sustain us in doing your will. Bless us with the presence of your Spirit in this moment of communion and throughout the weeks and years of our lives. Amen.

PRAYER FOR THE CUP: Gracious and self-giving God, help prepare our selfish and frightened hearts to receive your overflowing love. Open our eyes to glimpses of your presence everywhere. Open our hearts to the needs of others. Open our souls so that we may receive your compassion, poured out for us in Christ's self-giving love. May this cup we drink fill our lives with your Spirit, so that we might receive this self-giving love and learn to love others as you have loved us. Amen.

UNIFIED PRAYER: Prepare our hearts for the coming of our Savior, dear God. Straighten out the rough places in our attitudes; fill with your love the low places of fear and depression; tear down the hills of prejudice and pride. Here at this table may our spirits commune with your Spirit, so that your Spirit may touch and influence our lives. Bless this bread, so that in eating of it we may participate in Christ's body, given for us. Bless this cup, so that in drinking it we may participate in Christ's self-giving love, poured out for us. Guide our feet on the paths of peace. Amen.*

PRAYER AFTER COMMUNION: Faithful God, you have always been true to the covenants you have given your people. From the time of Abraham, you have sent prophets to call us to remember your tender mercies. In the fullness of time, you sent Jesus Christ to give us the knowledge of salvation and the forgivesness of sins. At this table of communion we have been called from darkness into light and have participated in the covenant of love that Christ instituted for us. May the light of your love continue to guide us in this Advent season. Amen.

*Dixon, *Everlasting Light*, pp. 55–56.

Third Sunday of Advent

Zephaniah 3:14–20
Isaiah 12:2–6
Philippians 4:4–7
Luke 3:7–18

PRAYER FOR THE BREAD: In a world of hatred, O God, you invite us to eat the bread of love. In a world of inequity, you invite us to eat the bread of justice. In a world of fear, you invite us to eat the bread of joy. In this Advent season, we come, daring to accept the living bread that you invite us to eat. Transform us by your Spirit, so that in eating this bread we may bind ourselves to the Christ whom you send. Amen.

PRAYER FOR THE CUP: We sing your praises, dear God, for you have given us salvation. We have drunk from the well of living water; you have filled our lives with joy. As we gather at this communion table in this time of preparation, we drink deeply of the love poured out for us in Jesus Christ. Open our hearts that we might realize the depth of your love for us and for all the human family. Let us learn from what we experience here how to love one another as you love us. Amen.

UNIFIED PRAYER: God of justice and love, how easy it is to stray from the paths you have set before us. Prejudice, fear, self-righteousness, and greed tempt us. Yet when we stray, you call us back through your prophets and through your word. We come to this table seeking to be true to your way. With repentant hearts, we eat the bread and drink the cup that you have given us. Help us learn to be more faithful and more loving. Open our hearts, so that we may receive the Christ you send us. Guide us by your Spirit that we may stay on your paths. Amen.*

PRAYER AFTER COMMUNION: Here at your table, dear God, we have experienced something of the peace that passes all understanding. May your peace continue with us as we go into the world. Amen.

*Dixon, *Everlasting Light*, p. 58.

Fourth Sunday of Advent

Micah 5:2–5a
Luke 1:47–55 or *Psalm 80:1–7*
Hebrews 10:5–10
Luke 1:39–45 (46–55)

PRAYER FOR THE BREAD: Our spirits rejoice in you, O God our savior. You have lifted us up from despair. You have filled us with good things. You have given your children the promise of peace and love. This bread that we eat is a sign of your generous love and a reminder of the one you sent to feed a hungry world, Jesus Christ. As we receive this bread, help us receive also the Christ, who came to show us your tender mercy. Direct us by your Spirit. Amen.

PRAYER FOR THE CUP: We have lived too long in darkness, O God of light and life. Greed and fear, selfishness and narrowness have dimmed our vision. We pray that through the light of Jesus Christ a new dawn will break, upon the world and upon us. As we anticipate the birth of Christ, may this cup recall for us that wonderful gift of love. In drinking it, we affirm that your love was poured out for us for our salvation. As we attempt to live as Christians, may your Spirit guide our feet on the paths of peace. Amen.

UNIFIED PRAYER: Shepherd us, dear God. Guide us and protect us. Prepare our hearts to be open to the love that you have to give. Bring to our hearts the joy of knowing your promise, the promise fulfilled in Jesus Christ our Savior. We come to your table to eat the bread and drink the cup that remind us why Christ came to earth. Bless us with your Spirit's presence as we receive the precious gift of love. Amen.*

PRAYER AFTER COMMUNION: We have come to your table, gracious God so that we might know more fully the one you have sent to us, Jesus Christ. As we go, guide us in your peace, that Christ's love might be born in us. Amen.

*Dixon, *Everlasting Light,* p. 61.

Christmas Eve/Christmas Day

Isaiah 9:2–7   *Isaiah 62:6–12*   *Isaiah 52:7–10*
Psalm 96   *Psalm 97*   *Psalm 98*
Titus 2:11–14   *Titus 3:4–7*   *Hebrews 1:1–4 (5–12)*
Luke 2:1–14   *Luke 2:(1–7) 8–20* *John 1:1–14*
(15–20)

(Any of the above scriptures may be used
on Christmas Eve or Christmas Day)

PRAYER FOR THE BREAD: God of life and light, we come to this table remembering the birth of Jesus Christ, the one you sent to be the bread of the world. As we eat the bread of communion, help us grow closer to Christ. Help us be nourished and strengthened by your love. As our savior was born in Bethlehem, let your Spirit be born in our hearts. Amen.

PRAYER FOR THE CUP: On this night (day) of beauty and holiness, we gather to reflect on the meaning of your love. You are a mighty God, yet you chose to express yourself through the power of vulnerability. You laid aside your glory that we might know your tender love. We see your self-giving nature in the babe in the manger and in the savior at the table in the upper room. In drinking this cup, we commit ourselves to your love and to the one in whose life your love is uniquely expressed. May your Spirit be our guide—to Bethlehem, to the upper room, to the cross, to the open tomb, and to the living Christ, who is in our midst. Amen.

UNIFIED PRAYER: You spoke the word, Creator God, and the universe came into being. You spoke the word, and life filled our planet. You spoke the word, and people received the covenant and the law to guide them. Tonight (today) we remember that you spoke the word, and the word became flesh, and dwelt among us. We thank you for the Christ who came into our presence as a baby, grew up, walked among us, healed, taught, and offered his life for us. The bread we eat reminds us that Christ is our living bread. The cup we drink helps us recall the love that was poured out for us in Christ's birth, life, and death. Yet this is more than a memorial; it is a celebration that the Christ who came into our midst became the risen Christ and is here with us. We rejoice in your word that made us, that came to us, and that is with us now. Fill us with your Spirit on this Christmas Eve (Day). Amen.*

STATEMENT AFTER COMMUNION: Go in peace. The baby in the manger, the teacher at the table, the savior on the cross, the victor of the open tomb has come into the world and is with us now.

*Dixon, *Everlasting Light,* pp. 64–65.

First Sunday after Christmas

1 Samuel 2:18–20, 26
Psalm 148
Colossians 3:12–17
Luke 2:41–52

PRAYER FOR THE BREAD: All creation praises your name, loving God. We praise and thank you for the precious gift of Jesus Christ, whose presence we celebrate in the breaking of bread today. Let us be aware that the living Christ who came to Bethlehem, whom we meet at this table, is with us every day. Guide us by your Spirit in the paths of holiness. Amen.

PRAYER FOR THE CUP: Wise God, teach us to walk the paths of wisdom. Give us hearts and minds eager to learn your ways. Help us grow in your Spirit. As we drink together from the cup that symbolizes Christ's love poured out for us, draw us closer to you and to one another. Amen.

UNIFIED PRAYER: Teach us your ways, O God of wisdom. Help us remember that no matter how young or old we are, we can still grow in faith, love, and grace. Let this table be a place where we can learn the ways of Christ. Let the bread we eat and the wine we drink help us learn that the boy in the temple became the man in the upper room. Through your Spirit, help us celebrate the presence of the living Christ with us. Amen.*

PRAYER AFTER COMMUNION: As we go from this table, gracious Host, let the word of Christ dwell in us richly; help us learn your wisdom; let our hearts be filled with gratitude and praise. Amen.

*Dixon, *Everlasting Light,* p. 68.

Second Sunday after Christmas

Jeremiah 31:7–14
Psalm 147:12–20
Ephesians 1:3–14
John 1:(1–9) 10–18

PRAYER FOR THE BREAD: Loving and wise God, it was your word that created the world. It was your word that gave the law and inspired the prophets. Then, because you heard our need, it was your word that took on human flesh in Jesus Christ and dwelled in our midst. As we take this bread, we remember the Christ who came to us as a human, to dwell with us, to die for us, and to bring us the gift of life. May your Spirit draw us ever closer to the living Christ. Amen.

PRAYER FOR THE CUP: During this season of Christmas, we remember especially that "the Word became flesh and lived among us" as we continue our celebration of your Son's birth. Help us to see your Son's glory, full of grace and truth. In drinking from the cup this day, help us feel your love for us, undeserved, filled with grace. Help us act as your children in our lives. Amen.

UNIFIED PRAYER: From everlasting to everlasting, you indeed have been our God. You have been with us from the beginning of creation; you sought us from all parts of the earth because you cared for us—your people. You adopted us as your heirs through your Son, Jesus Christ. Through Jesus Christ you have given us this bread and this cup, which are set before us today. We remember your great gift to us as we take these emblems today. Help us to live for the praise of Christ's glory as we give thanks to you. Amen.

STATEMENT AFTER COMMUNION: Because of our belief in God and God's Son, Jesus Christ, our lives are characterized by the joy of hope and an awareness of the richness of God's grace. This is a gift from God that shows a new way of living.*

*Marion Soards, Thomas Dozeman, and Kendall McCabe, *Preaching the Revised Common Lectionary, Year A: Advent/Christmas/Epiphany* (Nashville: Abingdon Press, 1992), p. 95, paraphrased.

Epiphany

Isaiah 60:1–6
Psalm 72:1–7, 10–14
Ephesians 3:1–12
Matthew 2:1–12

PRAYER FOR THE BREAD:
"Come Blessed Bread
We are hungry.
Nourish us with your presence
strengthen us to serve
enable us to forgive
inspire us to pray
and encourage us to share
the feast of your love,
a banquet for all."*

PRAYER FOR THE CUP: On this festive day, we celebrate the message that you planned for us—that Christ came for all people. You did not forget your people in bondage; you rescued them and restored them as your people. We praise you. You sent your Son, Jesus Christ, for all. For those who came to seek Jesus from far away, we praise you. You gave us the gift of your Son so that we might live eternally with you. We praise you. We drink together from this cup, which reminds us of this wonderful plan you have for us. We praise you. Amen.

*Janice K. Stanton, *The Secret Place* (Valley Forge, Penn.: American Baptist Churches in the U.S.A. Educational Ministries, 1999), p. 29.

UNIFIED PRAYER: Creator of Heaven and Earth, you have revealed yourself in your Son, Jesus Christ, our light and salvation. "You sent a star to guide the Magi to where the Christ was born; and your signs and witnesses in every age and through all the world have led your people from far places to his light."* On this day of Epiphany, we celebrate the coming of those who sought a savior. In eating this bread and drinking from this cup, we celebrate that we know a savior, Jesus Christ. In the presence of the Holy Spirit, let us commune in the light of the Word. Amen.

PRAYER AFTER COMMUNION: Gracious God, here at this table we have been in the company of Jesus Christ, our savior and redeemer. You have revealed your loving ways to us in broken bread and poured cup. Now as your light has illuminated our lives, help us be a light for others. Amen.

*Hoyt Hickman et al., *The New Handbook of the Christian Year* (Nashville: Abingdon Press, 1992), pp. 86ff.

First Sunday after Epiphany

Isaiah 43:1–7
Psalm 29
Acts 8:14–17
Luke 3:15–17, 21–22

PRAYER FOR THE BREAD: Your Holy Spirit is promised to us just as it was given to your Son, Jesus Christ, and to the disciples. We know that we receive this gift as we accept Jesus as our savior and are baptized by your living water. In the presence of the Holy Spirit we then come to your table to eat this living bread, the body of our Lord, Jesus Christ. Let us remember our commitment to you and our baptism as we share this bread. Amen.

PRAYER FOR THE CUP: We praise you, O God of Loving Power, as we come to your table this day. We know you are a powerful God. We know you are a loving God. You redeemed your people; you have given us a savior, Jesus Christ. This cup, in memory of his life, given for us, shows us your love. From this cup we have strength and peace in your holy name. Amen.

UNIFIED PRAYER: O great and merciful God, you watch over each of us as we are born. You care for us in all times of our lives. And you must rejoice greatly for each of us as we accept your Son, Jesus Christ, as our savior and are baptized in his name. As the waters of baptism wash over us, so your Holy Spirit washes over each of us now in coming to this table. We eat this bread and drink from this cup remembering our baptism and our commitment to live a life of discipleship. Give us strength to do your work. Amen.

PRAYER AFTER COMMUNION: This day, in celebrating the Lord's supper, we have been reminded of our baptism. With the help of the Holy Spirit, let our journey of formation and discipleship continue. Amen.

Second Sunday after Epiphany

Isaiah 62:1–5
Psalm 36:5–10
1 Corinthians 12:1–11
John 2:1–11

PRAYER FOR THE BREAD: We come to your table this day, God, as people of many different talents and gifts. Some of us can preach and teach, some can heal, and some can discern wisdom. Others of us can pray, while some can lead others to you. We thank you for these gifts of the Holy Spirit working together for the common good. The bread that we are about to take and share among us is also a sign of your gift of life eternal. You gave us your Son, Jesus Christ, in whom we find this life. In the eating of this bread, we acknowledge our gifts of the Spirit and promise to use them for the common good of your reign. Amen.

PRAYER FOR THE CUP: How precious is your steadfast love, O God! All people can take refuge in the shadow of your wings. We can feast upon the abundance of your house; you give us drink from the river of your delights. At this table today we drink from the cup of life given to us again by your steadfast love, God. We drink from the cup Jesus shared with the disciples in that upper room. This cup symbolizes not only your steadfast love but your faithfulness, righteousness, judgment, and salvation in Jesus Christ. In the presence of your Holy Spirit, we come to drink from this cup. Amen.

UNIFIED PRAYER: O God, the majority of our everyday lives are ordinary. We go about our work, play, and responsibilities. Yet every so often, a miracle happens. An early flower pokes its way through the snow. A child is born. A friend professes her faith in you. The dough rises to be baked into bread. The water is turned into wine. The bread and cup set before us tell us of the miracle of the resurrection of Jesus Christ. Just as the water jars were filled with water and then turned into wine, fill us with your Holy Spirit, changing our lives so that in the taking of the bread and cup we may experience the miracle of your love. Amen.

PRAYER AFTER COMMUNION: At this table we have communed with one another and with the living Christ. We praise God for giving us this opportunity. As we eat and drink in the week ahead, help us remember that then, too, we eat and drink with the living Christ. Amen.

Third Sunday after Epiphany

Nehemiah 8:1–3, 5–6, 8–10
Psalm 19
1 Corinthians 12:12–31a
Luke 4:14–21

PRAYER FOR THE BREAD: We come before you this morning at the table that is set for us. We break the bread, made by human hands. We will eat this bread in remembrance of our savior, Jesus Christ. And yet we know this bread is but one of the symbols of your riches, God. We seek your word, your truths, and your laws. As we share the bread, let us rejoice that we know you, O Lord and Savior. Let our words be acceptable to you. Amen.

PRAYER FOR THE CUP: We cannot come to this table, O Lord, to drink of this cup without remembering our Savior's life, death, and resurrection. We know that Christ came to fulfill your law. As we drink of this cup, let Christ's words challenge us to be your word in the world, proclaiming also the year of the Lord's favor. Amen.

UNIFIED PRAYER: Like the Israelites of old, we rejoice in the hearing of your word, O Lord. Help us listen also for understanding. Move us this day with the holiness of your words. As we eat this bread and drink from this cup, let us rejoice in your words of love, which came in Christ. Help us find ways to share with others not only your word but also the bread that gives nourishment to the body. Amen.

PRAYER AFTER COMMUNION: Kindle the flame of your Spirit that was lit in our souls at this communion table, dear God, that in the week ahead others may see your light and love in our lives. Amen.

Fourth Sunday after Epiphany

Jeremiah 1:4–10
Psalm 71:1–6
1 Corinthians 13:1–13
Luke 4:21–30

PRAYER FOR THE BREAD: God of all ages, you have called your children to faith, to trust in your way. You have called your children to hope by being trustworthy to your promises. You have called your children to love through the example of our Savior Jesus Christ. As we break and eat this bread today, help mold us into a community that reflects the faith, hope, and love to which you have called us. Help us live in the bonds of love, the bonds of your Spirit. Amen.

PRAYER FOR THE CUP: God of the prophets, we come to this table knowing that it can be an uncomfortable place. When we prefer to live for ourselves and for others just like us, you point out a hungry, suffering world and call us to love and serve it. When we prefer to feel good, you make our consciences hurt and twinge. As we drink this cup, help us remember that Christ drank the cup of suffering to free the world from sin's burden. By your Spirit, cure our self-imposed lack of vision and help us see what you would have us see—the living Christ who calls us to serve. Amen.

UNIFIED PRAYER: Lord of love, you have invited us to this table to learn your ways. You have set before us Jesus Christ to teach us a love that is steadfast and true. Even in the darkest of times, as they gathered in the upper room, Jesus taught the disciples your way of life, the love that is built into the very fabric of the universe. In giving them the bread, he taught them about how you provide bread for your hungry children. In giving them the cup, he taught them of your outpouring love that sealed the new covenant. As we eat and drink at this table, help us to learn, as you helped the first disciples. May your Spirit focus our minds and hearts on the love that you have given us, the love you want us to learn and share. Amen.

PRAYER AFTER COMMUNION: We have come to the table of Christ's love. Here we have found a love unconditional and pure. May the love that we have experienced here transform our lives as we go from this place, that we may be agents of Christ's love here in this community. Amen.

Fifth Sunday after Epiphany

Isaiah 6:1–8 (9–13)
Psalm 138
1 Corinthians 15:1–11
Luke 5:1–11

PRAYER FOR THE BREAD: We give you thanks with our whole hearts, loving God, because you have protected and preserved your people. You have given us glimpses of your glory, that we might honor you. You have revealed your nature to us through Jesus Christ, that we might love you. You have called us through Jesus Christ, that we might follow you. Here at this table, we offer bread that humans have made from the grain that you have provided. Yet in this simple act of taking and eating bread, we remember that Jesus Christ is the living bread. Turn our hearts to Jesus. Through your grace, help us experience the living Christ in our lives. Amen.

PRAYER FOR THE CUP: God of grace, in you we find life and hope, purpose and power. Through Jesus Christ, you call us to serve you and proclaim your good news. Help us respond faithfully and enthusiastically to your call. We gather around your table now to remember and proclaim the living Christ. As we raise and bless this cup, we witness that Christ poured out his life for us. As we drink from this cup, we affirm that his death was not in vain. Fill us with your Spirit, that we may know the presence of the living Christ in our midst. Amen.

UNIFIED PRAYER: Holy, holy, holy are you, God of light. The whole earth is full of your glory. We are a weak and sinful people, often driven by selfishness, hate, and fear, yet you have mercy on us. You call us to service and to faithfulness. Through Jesus Christ, we discover your nature and learn of your love. At this table we meet you and experience your forgiving nature. Here we eat the bread and remember Jesus Christ and his earthly ministry. Here we drink the cup and remember that Christ gave up his life on the cross but later conquered death so that we might know what it is to live in your Spirit. Bless us as we eat and drink; bless us as we remember Christ. Bless us with your Spirit, that we may be empowered to witness to our faith in word and deed. Amen.

PRAYER AFTER COMMUNION: You have called us to be your people, dear God. You have fed us and strengthened us at Christ's table. Now we pray that you will send us into the world as witnesses to your glorious name. Amen.

Sixth Sunday after Epiphany (Proper 1)

Jeremiah 17:5–10
Psalm 1
1 Corinthians 15:12–20
Luke 6:17–26

PRAYER FOR THE BREAD: Teacher God, we come here to learn your ways. We come because we know that your ways bring life and hope. Be patient with us when we learn slowly, when we put our trust in our own resources rather than in you. At this table we meet the living Christ and learn to trust your love. In eating this bread, we acknowledge our spiritual dependence on you. Open our hearts and help us grow in your Spirit. Amen.

PRAYER FOR THE CUP: When we depend on our own ways, gracious God, we dry up spiritually and live empty and meaningless lives. Here at this table we receive your invitation to sink our roots deep into your love and to be nourished by your grace. As we drink this cup, we remember Jesus Christ, the living water who came to give us life. In drinking it, may we flourish in your Spirit like trees beside the living water. In the life-giving name of Christ we come. Amen.

UNIFIED PRAYER: Creator God, you are the source of all life! Your love and creative power move through your whole creation, and through us. You have made all life interdependent. We cannot live unto ourselves alone, but depend on the food that ultimately you provide. As we come to this table, we realize that we are dependent on you for life, for meaning, and for purpose. How wonderful it is that you have sent us Christ. In coming to this table, we remember and affirm the living Christ in our midst. The bread that we break is a gift of your love, for in it we remember that Christ's body is offered for us. The cup from which we drink is also a gift of your love, for in it we remember how your love was poured out for us as the blood of Christ was poured out so that we might be part of your family. It is in your Spirit that we gather. It is in your Spirit that we live. Amen.

PRAYER AFTER COMMUNION: Life-giving God, we have been blessed to be here. Help us remember that we are part of the body of Christ on earth, so we can be a blessing to others. Help us to be filled with a lively hope, for this table just offers a glimpse of what is to come when we gather in your joy, glory, and love. Amen.

Seventh Sunday after Epiphany (Proper 2)

Genesis 45:3–11, 15
Psalm 37:1–11, 39–40
1 Corinthians 15:35–38, 42–50
Luke 6:27–38

PRAYER FOR THE BREAD: Your word is filled with instructions for living our lives in a Christlike way. You have told us to love our enemies; do good to those who do not like us; bless the ones who say bad things about us; and pray for those who abuse us. We are to give to those who take from us and also give to all who ask of us. We are asked to treat all your children as we would like to be treated. These are difficult things for us to do, O God. But you have shown us that it can be done by giving us your Son, Jesus Christ, who lived that kind of life. He also died being merciful to us.

This bread that we now eat reminds us of Christ's body, which he gave for us. By remembering his gift of life, we can choose to follow the instructions we are given. Amen.

PRAYER FOR THE CUP: You have told us to trust you and do good and we will receive justice. You have instructed us to be patient and not worry about those who do evil. You have asked us not to be angry, to put away wrath and not to worry, for you will put away those who do evil. We will try to follow your instructions, O wise God, for we know the rewards of those who follow you.

This cup on the table is one of the rewards of following you. You gave us your Son, who gave his very life for us. Our salvation is in Jesus Christ. We drink from this cup in praise to you. Amen.

UNIFIED PRAYER: On the cross, Jesus forgave the thief who asked to be pardoned. We know that you, God, have forgiven us of our sins, freeing us to be with you eternally. Yet it is harder for us to forgive those who have sinned against us. We harbor grudges and remember the wrongs that have been done against us by our brothers and sisters. We ask you to help us follow the example of Jesus Christ and forgive.

This table is a reconciling table where we all come, forgiven. As we share this meal together, let us do it as forgiving and forgiven people. The bread and cup are the signs of your forgiveness; our prayers are the signs of our forgiveness toward others. Amen.

PRAYER AFTER COMMUNION: Here at your table, dear Christ, we have been strengthened and refreshed to go into the world and do your mission. May the love that we have experienced here be a foretaste of the love we will all one day experience in your presence. Amen.

Eighth Sunday after Epiphany (Proper 3)

Isaiah 55:10–13
Psalm 92:1–4, 12–15
1 Corinthians 15:51–58
Luke 6:39–49

PRAYER FOR THE BREAD: Too often, O God, we come to your table somberly instead of joyously. Help us to approach this table with songs and praise for you who have delivered us to yourself.

We praise you for your Son, Jesus Christ, who gave his own self joyously for each one of us. With the eating of this bread, we remember your deliverance by his death and resurrection. Let us now go with joy to proclaim Christ's name. Amen.

PRAYER FOR THE CUP:

"Lord, by your wounds on Calvary
from death's dread sting your servants free,
that we may live eternally. Alleluia!"*

We are at your table Eternal God, to celebrate life eternal in you. The cup from which we drink is testimony to freedom from death, which you gave us in Jesus Christ. Alleluia. Amen.

*"The Strife is O'er," Latin hymn (1695), trans. Francis Pott, 1861.

UNIFIED PRAYER:

"As bread that was scattered on the hillside
was gathered together and made one,
so too, we, your people,
scattered throughout the world,
are gathered together around your table
and become one.
As grapes grown in the field
are gathered together and pressed into wine,
so too are we drawn together
and pressed by our times to share a common lot
and are transformed into your lifeblood
for all.
So let us prepare to eat and drink
as Jesus taught us:
inviting the stranger to our table
and welcoming the poor.
May their absence serve to remind us
of the divisions this eucharist seeks to heal.
And may their presence help transform us
into the body of Christ we share."*

STATEMENT AFTER COMMUNION: Thanks be to God, who gives us the victory through our Lord Jesus Christ (1 Cor. 15:57).

*Adapted from the Didache, quoted in Janet Schaffran and Pat Kozak, *More than Words* (Oak Park, Ill: Meyer Stone Books, 1986), p. 51.

Last Sunday after Epiphany

Exodus 34:29–35
Psalm 99
2 Corinthians 3:12—4:2
Luke 9:28–36 (37–43)

PRAYER FOR THE BREAD: We thank you, God, for your spiritual nourishment, for the richness of your reign, and for your comfort in our times of distress. Give us strength in times when it is difficult to witness to your Son, Jesus Christ. Help us learn to trust Christ and be willing to give our lives for Christ. For only as we do that will we find new life. We are confident that you will bless us as we confess Christ and walk in his paths. We celebrate this blessing as we take this bread, knowing that your Son was witness to your great love, even when it meant giving his very life. This bread, Christ's body, points to the risen Christ. Let us eat and be strengthened in our faith. Amen.

PRAYER FOR THE CUP: God of beauty and light, shine upon our lives. Transform us from sinful, selfish, and half-hearted followers into living witnesses to your glory. Help us remember that the Christ who is our friend, who meets us at this table, is also the transfigured and glorified Christ, shining by the light of your glory. We drink this wine to remember the Christ whose love saves and transfigures us all. Bless us as we drink it, through the power of your Spirit. Amen.

UNIFIED PRAYER: O God, you call us to be faithful, to be steadfast in our faith. We know our faith is first rooted in you and then in Jesus Christ. Help us to trust you and your ways and to be able to see your glory in the beauty of Christian lives. We come to the table in thanksgiving, celebrating the fruits of your love—this bread and cup—given to us by your grace. We celebrate the transfigured Christ, the suffering Christ, and the risen Christ as we eat and drink together. Bless us by your Spirit. Amen.

STATEMENT AFTER COMMUNION: We have come to the table of Jesus Christ and have been fed and strengthened. We have eaten at this table with the one who is our host. Let us praise God's great and awesome name.

First Sunday in Lent

Deuteronomy 26:1–11
Psalm 91:1–2, 9–16
Romans 10:8b–13
Luke 4:1–13

PRAYER FOR THE BREAD: For generations, Lord, we have heard your words telling us that we are your people. Yet we confess that we are tempted by other gods of power and possessions, of time and responsibilities. As we come to your table ready to eat the bread that reminds us of your Son Jesus Christ's body, forgive us our sins of leaning toward the temptations of life. Let us serve only you, our one true God. In acceptance of your forgiveness, we share this bread in the presence of the Holy Spirit. Amen.

PRAYER FOR THE CUP: Generous God, who has given us your Son, Jesus Christ, forgive us when we offer you our second best. We know we must offer to you our firstfruits in all parts of our lives, yet so often you get our leftover time, energy, and money. The cup we will drink is the firstfruit of your love for us, the blood of your Son. Thank you for such love offered for us. As we drink this cup today and always, help us to be reminded to offer you our firstfruits. Amen.

UNIFIED PRAYER: What a generous God you are! In days long ago, you delivered the children of Israel from slavery and brought them to a land flowing with milk and honey. Throughout the years, your Spirit has provided your children strength and sustenance when they have been weak, fearful, and tired. In Jesus Christ, you poured out your self-giving love that we might have life. As we share this bread, we find here a reminder of the true bread of life, given to us in Christ Jesus. As we share in this cup, we see a symbol of that love offered up on Calvary, and of your love offered now. Let your word guard us and guide us; let it be on our lips and on our hearts, that we may give you the glory now and forever. Amen.

STATEMENT AFTER COMMUNION: You, God, are our refuge and strength, our help in times of trouble. As we leave this meal of thanksgiving, help us be aware that we do not leave you here, but that your care and love surround us always. In Christ's name we pray and seek to live.

Second Sunday in Lent

Genesis 15:1–12, 17–18
Psalm 27
Philippians 3:17–4:1
Luke 13:31–35 or *Luke 9:28–36*

PRAYER FOR THE BREAD: Thank you, Lord, for asking, encouraging, and challenging us to trust and obey. You asked Abram to trust and obey you, and you did not disappoint him. Jesus trusted and obeyed you even to the cross.

This bread set before us that we will eat together represents the extent to which Jesus trusted and obeyed you. As we move from this table into the world, may trusting and obeying be part of our everyday lives. Amen.

PRAYER FOR THE CUP: O God of promise, we come to this table in anticipation of what you have done and can do for us. You have made us your people, you have protected us against our enemies, and you have given us heavenly citizenship and a savior, Jesus Christ. Set before us is the cup of these promises, filled with your love. The nourishment from this cup gives us power, vision, strength, and courage to live the Christian life. Amen.

UNIFIED PRAYER: God, as you helped Abram, help us to realize that there is more to life and living than meets the eye, that promises and possibilities exist beyond our human predicaments and limitations. This bread and this cup, the bread and body of our Lord, Jesus Christ, are so much more than mere earthly ingredients. They are the bread of promise and the cup of the ultimate possibility—life eternal with you in your love. Thank you for loving us. Amen.

STATEMENT AFTER COMMUNION: We have been to the Lord's table, and we rejoice. We have been in the presence of the living Christ, and we have been filled. We go now celebrating, because God is our light and our salvation.

Third Sunday in Lent

Isaiah 55:1–9
Psalm 63:1–8
1 Corinthians 10:1–13
Luke 13:1–9

PRAYER FOR THE BREAD:
"O let me feel thee near me!
The world is ever near;
I see the sights that dazzle,
the tempting sounds I hear;
my foes are ever near me, around me and within;
but, Jesus, draw thou nearer,
and shield my soul from sin."*

O loving God, we thank you for a savior to guide and keep us in your word and ways. The bread that we shall take gives us physical and spiritual strength to live as you have directed.

"O Jesus, thou hast promised to all who follow thee
that where thou art in glory there shall thy servant be;
and, Jesus, I have promised to serve thee to the end;
O give me grace to follow, my master and my
friend."**

We, your servants, nourished by this bread, go into the world to witness to your glory. Amen.

*John E. Bode, "O Jesus, I Have Promised" (1868).
**Ibid.

PRAYER FOR THE CUP: As we approach this holy table, we are thirsty for your presence. When we drink from your spiritual well, we are refreshed and fulfilled. This cup given to us in your greatest love, and made possible by the life, death, and resurrection of Jesus Christ, quenches our thirst for you eternally. Help us to bless you as long as we live. Amen.

UNIFIED PRAYER: O generous and giving God, you have invited those who thirst to come to the waters, and those who are hungry to come and eat. We can drink and eat without paying. Your spiritual food is free when we accept your covenant of love. Yet your Son, Jesus Christ, paid for us to be no longer thirsty or hungry by giving his life for each of us. Our thirst is quenched by this wine, our hunger by this bread. And our lives are bound to you in love, gratitude, and faithfulness. Amen.

PRAYER AFTER COMMUNION: God, send us forth from this table praising you for all that you have promised to us in your name. Amen.

Fourth Sunday in Lent

Joshua 5:9–12
Psalm 32
2 Corinthians 5:16–21
Luke 15:1–3, 11b–32

PRAYER FOR THE BREAD: O Giver of Bread, we are thankful for this holy place to come before you. You gave your people bread in the wilderness, sustaining them; now you give produce of the land. You have given us bread in the body of Jesus Christ, reconciling the world to yourself. You are present with us here now as we eat this bread. You have cared for your people through all generations. We feel the Holy Spirit's presence as we eat this bread. Amen.

PRAYER FOR THE CUP: We come to your table today, forgiving God, confessing that we have sinned against you and our neighbor. We know you will forgive us of these sins, restoring us to your holy grace. We again can become reconciled to you through Jesus Christ, who gave his life that we can be with you eternally. Let this cup that we drink remind us of this reconciling love and help us to sin no more. Guide our lives that we may live as ambassadors for Christ, being a channel for others to see you. Amen.

UNIFIED PRAYER: Like the father of the prodigal son, God, you have given us extravagant gifts of love. Like the father of the prodigal son, you have welcomed us back into your arms when we have turned from you. Like the father of the prodigal son, you have set a banquet table for us. In your providence and wisdom we are provided for as the Hebrews were long ago. In your providence and wisdom, you gave us a savior to reconcile us to you. We are recipients of all your lavish gifts.

We come now to your banquet table set with everything we need. The bread and wine satisfy us spiritually. With the help of the Holy Spirit, let us go into the world, reconciling others to you. Amen.

PRAYER AFTER COMMUNION: God, at this table we have felt your welcome home as we have strayed from you. We know you wait confidently for our return. We have felt your embrace as we celebrated this meal together. Whenever we come before you in communion, there is joy in heaven and on earth. Thanks be to God! Amen.

Fifth Sunday in Lent

Isaiah 43:16–21
Psalm 126
Philippians 3:4b–14
John 12:1–8

PRAYER FOR THE BREAD: Like Mary, who gave to your Son, without restraint, her costly gift of oil, anointing his feet, help us to give ourselves to you also without restraint. Let us not count the cost but dedicate ourselves to you, remembering all that you have done for us in your Son, Jesus Christ.

By his body, we are fed. This bread tells us of the great things you have done for us; as we eat it together, it reassures us that you will continue to feed us what we need. Holy Spirit, come, be with us as we come nearer to the time our Lord was crucified. Amen.

PRAYER FOR THE CUP:

"When I survey the wondrous cross
on which the Prince of glory died,
my richest gain I count but loss,
and pour contempt on all my pride.
Were the whole realm of nature mine,
that were a present far too small;
love so amazing, so divine,
demands my soul, my life, my all."*

God, your love is so amazing when we think of what you have given us in your Son, Jesus Christ. It is this

*Isaac Watts, "When I Survey the Wondrous Cross" (1707).

very wondrous cross that we celebrate at this table today, the cross of death, yet the cross of resurrection and life eternal in you. Help us to know the power of the resurrection and life in you as we drink from the cup made possible by this cross. Amen.

UNIFIED PRAYER: God of history, help us remember all that you have done for your people through the ages. Refresh our memories with the stories of your signs and wonders. But in all our *remembering*, let us keep before us not only what you have done but also what you are doing for us each time we come to this banquet table. We share the loaf and cup, the water in the desert and the manna in the wilderness. We share the Lord, Jesus Christ—a new way for all your people. Let us praise you, for you have done great things for us! Amen.

PRAYER AFTER COMMUNION: Forgiving God, we know that we did not come to this table because we deserve your love, but because we need your love. We did not come to be rewarded for our virtue, but to find forgiveness in your grace. Here we have experienced the presence of the one who died that we might live. Keep our hearts and minds open to the mystery we have experienced here. Amen.

Sixth Sunday in Lent (Palm Sunday)

Luke 19:28–40 and
Psalm 118:1–2, 19–29   or   *Isaiah 50:4–9a* and
Psalm 37:9–16

Philippians 2:5–11
Luke 22:14–23:56 or *Luke 23:1–49*

PRAYER FOR THE BREAD: In a world of superstars and media hype, we long for the one who can truly show us the way to life. Help us, dear God, to see that Jesus Christ is that one. When the noise has died down and the silence threatens us, may we feel the presence of Christ there with us, giving us support and encouragement. We come to this table today remembering that the broad daylight of the triumphal entry led through the dim light of the upper room to the darkness of the crucifixion. Then we realize what Christ meant when he said, "Take, eat, this is my body given for you." Open our hearts now to the one who longs to enter, so that we may be transformed by your love. Let your Spirit sustain us as we wait for the good news of resurrection. Amen.

PRAYER FOR THE CUP: There are those who would silence us, O living God, because our witness makes them uncomfortable. There is that within us that would keep us quiet, O God of the prophets, and draw us back from praising Christ. We, like your disciples of old, have moments of proud jubilation and moments of abject cowardice. Through the cup that we offer today, help us remember the living Christ who faced death that we might live. We lift our hearts and our souls to you. Through your Spirit may we be faithful disciples. Amen.

UNIFIED PRAYER: We open our hearts to you, O God of the living Christ. We sing our hosannas. We cry for you to save us. Enter our lives and fill us with the joy of your presence. As we begin this week of remembrance of your passion and death, focus our attention so that we may go beyond shallow praise to a deeper commitment. Give us the strength and courage to stay true to you in times of fear and temptation. Now we gather to break bread and to remember the price for which we have been bought. Now we gather to raise and drink from the cup and to remember the love that was poured out for us upon the cross. We thank you for bringing us here and pray that as we commune, our lives may be transformed to your service. Through Christ's spirit we pray. Amen.

PRAYER AFTER COMMUNION: Give thanks to God, whose steadfast love endures forever. Give praise to the living Christ, who is the ultimate expression of God's steadfast love. Give love to one another, just as you have received Christ's love at this table. Let your very lives shout out alleluia and hosanna. Amen.

Maundy Thursday

Exodus 12:1–4 (5–10), 11–14
Psalm 116:1–2, 12–19
1 Corinthians 11:23–26
John 13:1–17, 31b–35

PRAYER FOR THE BREAD: God, giver of light, you come to us in the midst of darkness, uncertainty, and brokenness, and we journey with you this evening. Even though we are in shadows of fear and aloneness, we sense your illuminating presence. On this sacred night, the loaf takes on new meaning as we ponder your Son's last few earthly days. We break the loaf; we know that as we observe this Holy Week, we commemorate Christ's broken body. We eat the bread; we proclaim the Lord's death until he comes. Come to us, Lord Jesus. Come, Holy Spirit, come. Amen.

PRAYER FOR THE CUP: Comforting God, this is a week in which we go from the triumphant celebration in Jerusalem, to the garden, to the cross. We go from celebration, to betrayal, to disbelief, to grief. Even though we experience this story with the eyes and memories of those who already know the Easter story, we still are discovering how God's resurrection will unfold in our lives.

We see this cup before us and, perhaps tonight more than any other time during the year, begin to realize its significance. We begin to internalize the power of your great love, God, as we hear again the story of our Savior's last days on earth. Let us sense your Holy Sprit's presence as we also journey to the cross. Amen.

UNIFIED PRAYER: We gather here this evening at the table of memories. Your Son, Jesus Christ, gives us, as he did the disciples, the gift of bread and wine to remember him by. He also gives us the gift of water, the waters by which we have seen Jesus weep, the waters of the sea where he and the disciples fished, the waters where our Savior taught. He gives us waters of new birth as we accept him as our Lord and Savior, and gives us the waters of our baptism.

This holy night we are given also the water in a basin that Jesus used to wash the feet of the twelve who sat with him in the upper room. Even as he washed their feet, he instructed them to be as servants, washing the feet of others.

As we go solemnly from this table, knowing what comes next in the drama of this Holy Week, help us keep the memories of the bread, wine, and water before us, giving us hope. Help us keep the meaning of the bread, wine, and water before us, that, with the help of the Holy Spirit, we may bring others to know you. And let the memory of the basin of water challenge us to be servants in your holy reign. Amen.

PRAYER AFTER COMMUNION:

> "'Tis midnight, and, for others' guilt,
> the Man of Sorrows weeps in blood;
> yet he that has in anguish knelt
> is not forsaken by his God.
> 'Tis midnight, and from heavenly plains
> is borne the song that angels know;
> unheard by mortals are the strains
> that gently soothe the Savior's woe."*

*William B. Tappan, "'Tis Midnight, and on Olive's Brow" (1822).

Easter Day

Acts 10:34–43 or *Isaiah 65:17–25*
Psalm 118:1–2, 14–24
1 Corinthians 15:19–26 or *Acts 10:34–43*
John 20:1–18 or *Luke 24:1–12*

PRAYER FOR THE BREAD: We have accepted your invitation this Easter Sunday to the table that you have prepared for us. Help us to see it in a new way. In the presence of the risen Christ, we are invited to see what has become dead in our lives in a life-giving way because of your great love. We have witnessed that death is not final; we have seen the risen Christ!

Help us to also see this ordinary bread in a new way, that it shows us the way of the risen Christ. Open our hearts that we may see and understand your love as shown to us in the resurrection of our Lord, Jesus Christ. Amen.

PRAYER FOR THE CUP: O God of ultimate surprises, we gather with joy at your table this Resurrection Day. The week has been long, as we have gone from Jerusalem, to the garden, to the cross, and to the tomb. Yet today the tomb is empty! Jesus has risen from the dead!

This cup of ordinary wine is ordinary no longer. It is the blood of the new covenant shed for each of us. We take it. We feel new life within us as we relive the resurrection story once again. God, we affirm again that your Word is indeed surprising and good! Amen.

UNIFIED PRAYER: What a contrast, Lord Jesus. The world screams about power and control, and you whisper, "I love you." The world yells about revenge and retribution, and you whisper, "I forgive you." The world teaches us to take all we can get, and you whisper, "Supper is ready. Come, share a meal with me...while I wash your feet."

Dear, dear Messiah, I will not let the cacophony of the world drown out your still, small voice. I hear your whispers calling me to Easter morn. I feel your resurrection embrace, and I know again that you are my risen Savior. Be alive in my life and make me your *Hallelujah*! Jesus, thank you for letting us share this holy meal. Amen.*

PRAYER AFTER COMMUNION: We have shared the bread and wine as Jesus taught. We know that with each time we share it and with each time we celebrate the resurrection, our lives are forever changed. Let us go forth and celebrate the good news! Amen.

*Contributed by Ben Bohren.

Second Sunday of Easter

Acts 5:27–32
Psalm 118:14–29 or *Psalm 150*
Revelation 1:4–8
John 20:19–31

PRAYER FOR THE BREAD: Father, we thank you for answering prayer and healing broken hearts. We know that where there is death, you can bring life. When you sent your Son, Jesus, it was to die that we might have new life. As we eat of this bread, the symbol of his broken body, may we receive the strength and courage to trust in his promise of everlasting life and to feel his love surrounding us. In his name we pray. Amen.*

PRAYER FOR THE CUP:
"Breathe on me, Breath of God; fill me with life anew,
that I may love what thou dost love,
and do what thou wouldst do."**

O God, your power and wonder are so great we can scarcely believe. Jesus Christ, firstborn of the dead, your Son, and our Savior are concepts beyond our comprehension. Yet you gave this gift to us. The cup set before us, which we will drink, is but a symbol of your great love. Breath of God, Holy Spirit, let our hearts swell with your love as we go into the world as your witnesses. Amen.

---

*Prayed at the communion table by Virginia Eaton, elder at Northside Christian Church, St. Louis, Missouri, the Sunday following her husband's funeral.
**Edwin Hatch, "Breathe on Me, Breath of God" (1878).

UNIFIED PRAYER: O Faithful One, we too often doubt your great love for us as shown in the life, death, and resurrection of your Son, Jesus Christ. We are like Thomas, wanting tangible proof, wanting to see before we believe. Help us in our doubting, help us to believe in faith. In coming to your table today, God, we see the bread and cup; we believe in faith, seeing the body and blood of our Savior. In the participation of this holy meal, we affirm our faith and belief in Jesus, the Messiah, the Son of God. Amen.

PRAYER AFTER COMMUNION: To him who loves us and freed us from our sins by his blood and made us to be a kingdom, priests serving his God and Father, to him be glory and dominion forever and ever. Amen (Rev. 1:5–6).

Third Sunday of Easter

Acts 9:1–6 (7–20)
Psalm 30
Revelation 5:11–14
John 21:1–19

PRAYER FOR THE BREAD: God of new life, we remember the dawn of a new day when the risen Christ stood on a lakeshore with Peter and the disciples, and he broke bread and gave it to them to eat. How thrilled they must have been to eat with their risen Lord, to know that he had overcome death. How moved they must have been when they recalled how in the upper room Christ had likewise broken bread and given it to them to eat. As we gather now, we celebrate that the risen Christ is in our midst as well. As we break the bread, share it, and eat of it, we do so in the faith that the living Christ is with us and that this, too, is the dawn of a new day of justice, peace, and love. Amen.

PRAYER FOR THE CUP: We gather at this table to remember Jesus as he poured the wine, blessed it, and gave it to the disciples, gathering them into a new covenant of life. As we drink this cup, we praise Christ in our hearts and look forward to the time when we can praise Christ, the worthy lamb, before the heavenly throne. To this living Christ and to you, O God, be blessing and honor and glory and might forever and ever. Amen.

UNIFIED PRAYER: Living God, living Christ, and living Spirit, open our hearts that we may recognize your presence in our midst. Let us eat this bread and drink this cup that you offer as a sign of Christ's presence. Open our eyes that we may see your glory, for you are great. Open our mouths that we might sing your praises, for you are worthy. Open our hands that we may serve others in love and mercy, for you are compassionate. As you have fed and cared for us in giving us this bread and this cup, so let us feed and care for others in your name. Amen.

PRAYER AFTER COMMUNION: At this table, gracious God, we have come into your presence and have received your blessing. Let us go from here nourished and strengthened, that we might be a blessing for others. In Christ's name we pray. Amen.

Fourth Sunday of Easter

Acts 9:36–43
Psalm 23
Revelation 7:9–17
John 10:22–30

PRAYER FOR THE BREAD: Shepherd God, we know you care for us as a shepherd cares for the sheep. You provide for our every need. You show us how to live. You protect us from all that would harm us. We are comforted by your presence.

We come to the table that you have prepared for us knowing that this bread is yet another way you care for us, for this bread reminds us of the body of your Son, Jesus Christ, who through your goodness and mercy gave his life for us. In taking this bread, we celebrate your reign on earth. Holy Spirit, come and empower us to live as witnesses to the resurrection! Amen.

PRAYER FOR THE CUP: Encompassing God, we come to your table today as a group of many kinds of people. Some of us are rich, some poor; some married, some single, some widowed. We are male, female; old, young, middle-aged. We represent many races and nationalities. Yet we know we all have a place at this table. We know that each one of us, like Lydia and Tabitha, can become a disciple of yours. And we are assured that your healing love is for each of us. By drinking from this cup, we witness to the wideness of your mercy given to us in the life, death, and resurrection of Jesus Christ. Amen.

UNIFIED PRAYER:

"Shepherd of souls, refresh and bless
thy chosen pilgrim flock
With manna in the wilderness,
with water from the rock.
Be known to us in breaking bread,
but do not then depart;
Saviour, abide with us, and spread
Thy table in our heart.
There sup with us in love divine;
Thy body and Thy blood,
That living bread, that heav'nly wine,
be our immortal food."*

PRAYER AFTER COMMUNION: We praise you this Eastertide for the new beginnings that this season brings. We praise you for love and deliverance.

Holy Spirit, show us your directives; give us hope and courage to follow, that God's reign will be in this place. Amen.

---

*James Montgomery, "Shepherd of Souls, Refresh and Bless" (1825).

Fifth Sunday of Easter

Acts 11:1–18
Psalm 148
Revelation 21:1–6
John 13:31–35

PRAYER FOR THE BREAD: O Lord Christ, you are the Alpha and Omega, the beginning and the end. As we gather to break bread at your table, we are reminded of your daily presence in our lives, sustaining us and supporting us. Here we receive a foretaste of the new heaven and the new earth that you have promised your children. Help us realize how awesome it is to be in your presence here, so that we may not take you for granted, but instead acclaim you as Lord of our lives. Open our hearts that we may receive your Spirit's blessing, and having received it, share it with others. Amen.

PRAYER FOR THE CUP: We come to your table a thirsty people, dear God. The finest wines the world offers cannot quench our thirst for meaning, joy, and hope. Only as we come to Christ, who is the living water, will we find that which truly satisfies. Here as we raise the cup of communion, we remember your promise that in the heavenly city we will be able to drink from the spring of the water of life. We know that you are trustworthy in your promises, but we are fearful and insecure. Help this cup be for us a reminder of your grace, that in the living Christ we may be refreshed. Strengthen us by your Spirit. Amen.

UNIFIED PRAYER: Dear God, you made us to be one. Yet many prejudices and fears separate us from one another. We are comfortable in our ways of worship, but we tend to suspect those who worship you in other ways. We are comfortable with Christians we know but we are quick to find fault in those we don't. You have created us in a rainbow of hues, but we too readily distrust and fear those whose skin is of a different shade. This table is a witness to the unity you desire for your people, but it is also a witness to our scandal of division. As we come to this time of communion, help us realize that you show no partiality, that you have called us all to be one in Christ. As we eat this bread and drink this cup, transform our minds and spirits with your love, so that we may see in a new way. Help us to show no partiality, but to witness to the entire world that we are all truly one in Christ Jesus. Amen.*

STATEMENT AFTER COMMUNION: We have come to this table to affirm the glory of our risen Lord, Jesus Christ. We have come to honor the one who loved all of us and who taught us that we should love one another. As we go back into our daily lives, may the love that we demonstrate show the world that we are Christ's disciples.

*This prayer is also appropriate for World Communion Sunday.

Sixth Sunday of Easter

Acts 16:9–15
Psalm 67
Revelation 21:10; 21:22–22:5
John 14:23–29 or *5:1–9*

PRAYER FOR THE BREAD: Be gracious to us and bless us, dear God. Help us know your presence with us today through the risen Christ. We lift our hearts to you in humility and trust, knowing that your love for us is true. We lift this bread before you, remembering that Jesus, before his death and resurrection, lifted bread and broke it so that we might remember his body given for us. We eat this bread in your presence, knowing that the living Christ is here with us. May your Spirit sustain us at this table and throughout our days, as a church and as individuals. Amen.

PRAYER FOR THE CUP: Your love, O God, is like a river that never runs dry. Your love refreshes us and gives us life. Here at this table, we celebrate the love that you gave us through Jesus Christ, who lived, died, and rose from the dead, so that we might know you and love you. As we drink from this cup, we celebrate your love that never runs dry. Help us learn the ways of Christ, who is the living water. Help us walk in the ways of the Spirit, that we may be your faithful people. Amen.

UNIFIED PRAYER: Come and stir our souls with your Spirit, great God of life. When we are paralyzed by fear or apathy, may we see the living Christ inviting us to be whole. We come to this table knowing that Christ is the living water, the healing presence, the caring friend that we need to help us onto our feet. Bless this bread and help us remember Christ as we partake. Bless this cup and help us know the awesome reality of a love that does not stop, even at the cross. We pray that as we are fed here, we may hear and discern your Spirit's call and will follow its lead to where you would have us go. Amen.

PRAYER AFTER COMMUNION: Let all the peoples praise you, O God; let all the peoples praise you. You have blessed us with life. You have blessed us with love. We have experienced your love at this table. Praised be your name. Amen.

Seventh Sunday of Easter

Acts 16:16–34
Psalm 97
Revelation 22:12–14, 16–17, 20–21
John 17:20–26

PRAYER FOR THE BREAD: You are the one God, and you call us to be one in Jesus Christ. You are the God of glory, and you have allowed us to see your glory in Jesus Christ. You are the God of love, and we have seen your love ultimately expressed through Jesus Christ. We gather at your table now to remember Jesus Christ as we eat bread. Help bring us together as we eat, overcoming those barriers that divide us. Unite us by your Spirit, so that we may truly be your people. Amen.

PRAYER FOR THE CUP: Through the power of your Spirit, gracious God, we have come. We are a thirsty people—our lives are dry, and our spirits are arid with lack of meaning. Here, at your invitation, we have come to take the water of life, Jesus Christ, as a gift. As we bless this cup, our hearts rise to you in grateful thanks for that gift. As we drink from this cup, your Spirit refreshes our spirits. May these moments of communion refresh and strengthen us, that in the week ahead we may live as you would have us live and love as you would have us love. Amen.

UNIFIED PRAYER: We come to this table, God of all creation, to celebrate the Alpha and the Omega, the Beginning and the End, our Lord, Jesus Christ. In Christ is our life. In Christ is our hope. In Christ is our strength. Here at this table, we affirm our faith in and celebrate our relationship with the bright morning star, Jesus Christ. In eating this bread, we remember that Christ came in human flesh to be God-with-us. In drinking this cup, we proclaim that the love that was poured out for us in Christ's death emerged triumphant. Bless us as we partake, that we might grow in your Spirit. Amen.

STATEMENT AFTER COMMUNION: The Spirit has led us to this place. The living Christ has fed us. Now we go with the knowledge that as God was here, so God will be with us as we go.

Day of Pentecost

Acts 2:1–21 or *Genesis 11:1–9*
Psalm 104:24–34, 35b
Romans 8:14–17 or *Acts 2:1–21*
John 14:8–17 (25–27)

PRAYER FOR THE BREAD: Gracious God, send us your Spirit. On this special day, the birthday of the church, we ask for wisdom and understanding that only the indwelling Spirit can give us. We pray that the church—all of us— will grow closer to one another in unity, and that we will work to serve you. Let your reign come in this world, where you have given each of us a task. For the bread that you have broken and given to us, for your words of love, for your forgiveness of our many sins, and for your promise to be with us always, we give you our grateful thanks. Amen.*

PRAYER FOR THE CUP: Pour your Spirit upon us, dear God. Let your love overflow in our hearts and in this congregation, that others might be amazed at the power of the Spirit and the living Christ. Wash away our apathy, fear, and indifference; purify us of our sin and selfishness; transform us by the power of your Spirit. In drinking from the cup of communion, may we realize the power of the love that was poured out for us on Calvary, the power of the Spirit that was poured out upon your church at Pentecost, and the power of the living Christ in our midst today. Amen.

*Adapted from a prayer by Ginni Bowie, Northside Christian Church, St. Louis, Missouri.

UNIFIED PRAYER: Forgive us, dear God, when we come to this table and expect nothing to happen. Focus us, nurturing God, when our attention wanders and we get distracted. Encourage us, loving God, when we are frightened or downhearted. Challenge us, life-giving God, to be alert to the workings of your Spirit, that we may allow it to touch us in the deepest parts of our lives. As your Spirit overwhelmed the believers at Pentecost and helped them all hear the good news of Jesus Christ, so we pray that your Spirit may work within and among us today. In eating this bread, in drinking this cup, may we feel the presence of the living Christ in our midst. Transform us, so that the world may see in you, through us, its hope and future. Amen.

PRAYER AFTER COMMUNION: Thank you, God, for inviting us to this table. Thank you for the presence and power of your Spirit. Help us live as your faithful people. Amen.

Trinity Sunday (First Sunday after Pentecost)

Proverbs 8:1–4, 22–31
Psalm 8
Romans 5:1–5
John 16:12–15

PRAYER FOR THE BREAD: God of wisdom, you have formed and shaped all creation, and you have formed and shaped us to be your children. When in our fear and selfishness we ignore you or try to run away, still you call us to come and share in your joy. Through Jesus Christ, you have invited us to this table that we might eat bread, be nourished, and come to know you better. Through your Spirit, you unite us here to be in peace and harmony with you and with one another. We praise your name as we accept your invitation. And as we eat this bread, accepting your invitation to come to this table, help us realize that we are inviting you into our bodies, our minds, our souls, and our hearts. Amen.

PRAYER FOR THE CUP: O God, our God, how wonderful are your works. Who are we that you should care for us? Yet we know that in Jesus Christ we have found access to your grace. As wine is poured into the cup, O Gracious God, your love is poured into our hearts through the Holy Spirit. Bless us now as we drink from this cup. Fill us with your grace. Through your Spirit, open our eyes that we may see the beauty of your holiness. Through your Spirit, open our minds that we may see Christ in our neighbors, even those we may now distrust and fear. Through your Spirit, open our hearts that we may love as you would have us love. Amen.

UNIFIED PRAYER: We praise you, O Creator God, for you are great and wonderful. Your wisdom and your love are written in the very fabric of creation. Your power and creativity are displayed in the galaxies. Yet you are as close to us as our heartbeats. In Jesus Christ, you have expressed your love for us, a love that never gives up, a love that never lets go. Bless us as we eat this bread and remember that Christ's body was given for us. Bless us as we drink this cup and remember that his blood sealed the new covenant for us. We thank you, dear God, for the presence of your Spirit, the Spirit that draws us close to you and to the living Christ. Through your Spirit, help us live as you would have us live. Amen.

PRAYER AFTER COMMUNION: Through your love, we were formed, O Creator God. Through Jesus Christ, we have entered into a saving relationship with you. Through your Spirit, we are one people of faith. At this table, we have experienced blessed companionship with you and with one another. Now as we go, help us live in such a way that your love and grace will be evident to the world around us. Amen.

Proper 4*
Sunday between May 29 and June 4
(if after Trinity Sunday)

1 Kings 18:20–21 (22–29), 30–39
Psalm 96
Galatians 1:1–12
Luke 7:1–10

PRAYER FOR THE BREAD: We sing to you a new song, dear God, because you are the one who makes us new. You are our hope and our strength. Without you, our lives are empty and meaningless; with you they are full and joyous. At this table, we remember that all good food, strength, and refreshment come from you. We are here because we remember Jesus Christ, who came to be the living bread, who came to heal and restore, who came to give us life. Guide us by your Spirit as we try to live, love, and serve in Christ's name. Amen.

PRAYER FOR THE CUP: We bless your name, O God of beauty and strength. Because of the power of your love, we have become your children. Be with us as we bless this cup, and as we remember the Christ who gave of himself to bring us into your family. May we remember the covenant that Christ established and turn away from the idols that would tempt us. Through your Spirit, help us live as your children, to bring healing to our relationships and to draw others to your love. Amen.

*For Propers 1–3, see pp. 32–37.

UNIFIED PRAYER: Gracious God, we can never be worthy enough to do that which we are about to do. We admit that we do not deserve to be invited to dinner at your house. Yet here at this table, you receive us, and Christ offers his body and blood for us. We do not have to pass a test; we do not have to earn our way and we do not have to pay for the privilege, for you in your grace have made us worthy. Bless us now as we bless these elements. Refresh us, restore us, and heal us as we partake. Guide us and challenge us as we try to live and witness in your name. Amen.

STATEMENT AFTER COMMUNION: Here at this table we have celebrated the one who has set us free from bondage to sin, Jesus Christ. Here we have gathered in Christ's name to be fed by Christ's spirit. From here we go, a free and holy people, to praise God and to love our neighbors.

Proper 5
Sunday between June 5 and 11
(if after Trinity Sunday)
1 Kings 17:8–16 (17–24)
Psalm 146
Galatians 1:11–24
Luke 7:11–17

PRAYER FOR THE BREAD: When we are hungry, gracious God, you give us food. When we are weak, you sustain us. When we are discouraged, you lift our spirits. As you are gracious, teach us to be trusting. In eating this bread, we remember the bread shared between a widow and a prophet, and we remember the bread shared between Jesus Christ and the disciples. Even in the shadow of death, bread became the symbol of life. Let it be a symbol today of the abundant life that you give through Jesus Christ. Through your Spirit, teach us at this table to be a sharing, caring people. Amen.

PRAYER FOR THE CUP: Come into our hearts, living Christ. We are not worthy to receive you, but you make us worthy by your very love. Sometimes our spirits feel shriveled and dying, our souls parched, but you give us living water. You refresh and renew your children. We come now to bless and drink this cup and to remember our Lord, Jesus Christ, who came to forgive and to heal. May your Spirit mold and shape our spirits, so that we may become a people of blessing. Amen.

UNIFIED PRAYER: We will praise you, O God, for you alone are worthy. You are our creator, our help, and our hope. You stand by those who are oppressed and give food to the hungry. You set prisoners free and give new vision when our eyes are clouded. Be our vision and guide, so that we may learn your ways and become a just, compassionate, caring people. Let this table be a learning place for us. As we eat the bread and drink the cup, may we learn to live as Christ would have us live. Amen.

PRAYER AFTER COMMUNION: Here at Christ's table, we learn of your generosity and graciousness, O God. As we go from this place, help us be gracious and generous too. Amen.

Proper 6
Sunday between June 12 and 18

1 Kings 21:1–10 (11–14), 15–21a
Psalm 5:1–8
Galatians 2:15–21
Luke 7:36–8:3

PRAYER FOR THE BREAD: We do not come here to celebrate our own righteousness, dear God, for we know that none of us measure up to your holiness. Rather, we come to this table knowing that through the sacrifice of Jesus Christ you have justified us. As we eat this bread, we are aware of your steadfast love for all your children. How abundant is your love, that we can come here and be fed by your Spirit! It brings us joy to be here in your presence, and it brings us peace to know that we are never far from you. Amen.

PRAYER FOR THE CUP: O generous God, you have given us your precious Son, Jesus Christ. You held back nothing, but gave willingly that we might know your love for us. We drink this cup together, remembering that tremendous sacrifice, that wonderful gift given in your love for us. Challenge us in our responsibility to be generous with the gifts you have given us. Let us not hold back, but give of our all with joy! Amen.

UNIFIED PRAYER: Many times we deceive others, O forgiving God; many times we try to deceive ourselves, and many times we try to deceive you. Here at your table, help us realize that we come not because of our own goodness, but because of our need. Help us by the power of your Spirit to see into our own hearts and open ourselves to your forgiving power. And as you have forgiven and accepted us, help us learn not to judge or look down on others. Through the bread we now break and the wine we now pour, remind us that Christ lives in us, cleansing, leading, and loving us. In Christ is our life. May we strive to live by faith through the Christ who loves us and who gave himself for us. Amen.

PRAYER AFTER COMMUNION: We have found refuge in your presence, dear God, and we rejoice in these moments of communion. As we return to our daily lives, help us remember Jesus Christ each time we break bread. Amen.

Proper 7
Sunday between June 19 and 25

1 Kings 19:1–4 (5–7), 8–15a
Psalms 42 and 43
Galatians 3:23–29
Luke 8:26–39

PRAYER FOR THE BREAD: O God, we seek you in many places and in many things. We look for you in the workplaces where we spend our days; we look for you in the malls and on the busy highways. We seek you in our homes, within our families. We search for you in our many possessions and pastimes. In the entire realm of nature, we are always waiting for you. Yet we know you are with us always in each place that we may be. You seek us and let us feel your presence. We feel you closest, God, at this table, when we gather to eat the bread that reminds us of the body of your Son, Jesus Christ. In the eating of this bread, we realize you have sought us always and made it possible to be with you always. Amen.

PRAYER FOR THE CUP: God of miracles, we come to this table confessing that we do not always give you thanks for the great and wonderful things you have done for us. It is too easy to go on our way, forgetting the source of our help. Help us to be more like the man Jesus healed of the demons, who then went about telling others how much Jesus had done for him.

The cup on this table is the representation of this great love—the blood of our savior given for us. As we drink of the cup, help us to know we are forgiven for not proclaiming what you have done for us. Give us the strength and courage to witness to your great love. Amen.

UNIFIED PRAYER: At this holy table, God, we are painfully aware that we have not followed, in faith, what you would have us do. Belief in you and even baptism in Christ still does not lead us to act as you would have us act. In you, all sisters and brothers are one; we have sinned in our making distinctions and separating one from another. Forgive us these sins; help us to see the unity of all your children. Even more, help us to act on the words that all are one in Christ Jesus. This table unifies all Christians. Let us eat and drink in celebration of the unity that Christ Jesus himself taught us. Amen.

PRAYER AFTER COMMUNION: Go forth proclaiming what God has done for God's people. Go forth proclaiming the miracles of Jesus; go forth proclaiming the unity of all peoples. Amen.

Proper 8
Sunday between June 26 and July 2

2 Kings 2:1–2, 6–14
Psalm 77:1–2, 11–20
Galatians 5:1, 13–25
Luke 9:51–62

PRAYER FOR THE BREAD: Guide us by your Spirit, dear God, that we might know your will for us. Teach us that we might learn from you. Open our hearts that we might receive your love. We gather at this table to remember your great works, and especially to remember the Christ whom you sent. Our hearts are filled with awe and wonder when we eat this bread, remembering that Christ gave his life for us. Through Christ, you have redeemed us and called us to be your people. Help us respond to your call and live as faithful disciples. Amen.

PRAYER FOR THE CUP: God of freedom, you created us to be free, to live lives of beauty and wholeness, of grace and power. Yet there is so much that would tempt us to give up our freedom for false security. Here, as we drink this cup, we remember the Christ who poured out his life that we might be free from sin and fear. In drinking the fruit of the vine, may we be filled with the fruit of your Spirit and live lives that show your presence. Amen.

UNIFIED PRAYER: Holy God, we come to this table aware of our own flawed natures, aware of all that separates us from you. Yet through Jesus Christ you have called us to discipleship. Through your Spirit you have nurtured and strengthened us. At this table, you feed us. Bless this bread and wine as we partake and help us realize the presence of the living Christ in our lives. May these moments of communion support and sustain us, that we may live as good and faithful disciples. We pray through the power of your Spirit. Amen.

STATEMENT AFTER COMMUNION: God has called us to lives of faithful discipleship. In our response to that call, we find true freedom. Here at this table we have received strength for our journey. Now, in the company of the risen Christ, we can go from this place and be God's people in the world.

Proper 9
Sunday between July 3 and 9

2 Kings 5:1–14
Psalm 30
Galatians 6:(1–6), 7–16
Luke 10:1–11, 16–20

PRAYER FOR THE BREAD: Your church is gathered in many different places and speaks many different languages, dear God. We affirm that we are one church, and you are one God. Yet we are tempted to set ourselves against one another, to believe that our ways alone are your ways. Help us realize that we all need to come to you to find our help and healing. Help us put aside our pride and prejudice and accept all your children as our brothers and sisters. The bread we now eat is symbolic of the body of Christ and a sign that Christ was willing to give of himself to heal our sin-sick souls. As we break this bread and eat, heal us of our selfishness and bind us together in love through the Spirit who unites us. Amen.

PRAYER FOR THE CUP: In you, O living God, our mourning has turned to dancing, and our grief into joy. For you are the God of resurrection power, of new beginnings, of undying faithfulness. We come to this table to celebrate your reign and to witness to your love. We pour now the cup of hope. In so doing, we remember that Christ's love was poured out for us and affirm that Christ's love is victorious over death. Fill our hearts with your Spirit, so that we may witness to others of your love through words and deeds of love. Amen.

UNIFIED PRAYER: We sing praises to you, living God, and we give thanks to your holy name. Thank you for calling us to be your disciples. Thank you for this table, for here we learn whom it is that we follow. Thank you for this meal, for in partaking of it, we are equipped to minister to others in Christ's name. We eat this bread and drink from this cup to reenact and remember the holy meal that Christ had with his disciples. Bless us in our eating and bless us in our drinking, so that we may become a blessing for others. Help us find here the strength that we need, so that we don't get weary or discouraged in bearing our witness to a needy world. May your Spirit guide us and bless us. Amen.

PRAYER AFTER COMMUNION: Thank you, God of peace, that in this noisy, conflicted world we have had these moments of silent reflection. Thank you, gracious God, that in a world of great demands on our time and energy, you have fed us. Thank you, living God, that in a world where there is such great need, you have called us to mission and ministry. Bless us as we go from this table. Amen.

Proper 10
Sunday between July 10 and 16

Amos 7:7–17
Psalm 82
Colossians 1:1–14
Luke 10:25–37

PRAYER FOR THE BREAD: Holy God, you created us *in* love and created us *to* love. Because of your love for us, you sent us Jesus Christ, that we might learn to love you, to love ourselves, and to love one another. In taking this bread, we remember the Christ you sent. Help us learn here Christ's way of love and compassion. By your Spirit and in Christ's name we pray. Amen.

PRAYER FOR THE CUP: God of life and hope, plant your word in our lives and let it bear fruit. Inspire us so that others may see the power of the risen Christ in us. As we drink from the fruit of the vine, may we remember the Christ who called us into new life. Open our minds, so that we might begin to comprehend the power of your grace, and open our spirits, so that grace may transform our lives. We pray in the name of the one who came to rescue us from the power of sin, Jesus Christ. Amen.

UNIFIED PRAYER: God of justice, God of compassion, we come before you seeking your mercy. Too often our lives are marked by selfish complacency. Too often we benefit materially from injustice and oppression. Too often we build barriers of indifference to protect us from the world's pain. Stir within us the spirit of the prophets and stir within us the spirit of Christ, so that we may know the beauty of transformed, compassionate, and just lives. Help us realize that at this table we are not only one with one another here, but that we are also one with all those over the whole world who cry out to you. In eating this bread, we satisfy a spiritual hunger by recalling the Christ who became the living bread. In drinking this cup, we satisfy a spiritual thirst by recalling the Christ who is the living water. With the strength, insight, and joy that we receive here, help us learn to reach out to others in Christ's name, as Christ has reached out to us. Amen.

PRAYER AFTER COMMUNION: In your generosity and compassion, dear God, you have fed us. As we rise from your table, give us compassionate and generous hearts that we might be able to go and feed others. Amen.

Proper 11
Sunday between July 17 and 23

Amos 8:1–12
Psalm 52
Colossians 1:15–28
Luke 10:38–42

PRAYER FOR THE BREAD: O Loving God, we know you want us to hear your words and, because of that hearing, act accordingly. We confess that we often act in ways that are unjust and selfish. Forgive us when we act and talk as though we do not know your ways. Help us to turn to Christ, your Son, and follow his teachings. This bread that we now take demonstrates your forgiveness, your giving of your Son for us. As we go, strengthened, we pray that we will always be eager to hear your words and follow your ways. Amen.

PRAYER FOR THE CUP: Providential God, you know that our need is to be one with you. You have made that possible through your only Son, Jesus Christ, whom you sent to us to be our savior. Through his life and death and resurrection, he has made all one with you. The cup on this table shows us the power of the cross, for by Christ's death we are healed; by Christ's resurrection, we are reconciled to you. We thank you for what you have done for us. Amen.

UNIFIED PRAYER: We come to you, mighty God, trusting in your steadfast love. We praise you for what you have done for us, your undeserving people. We give thanks for your Son, Jesus Christ, who came that we would have life eternal. This bread and cup that are on the table before us are earthly reminders of the riches you have in store for us. In sharing this meal today, we recommit our selves to you. Amen.

STATEMENT AFTER COMMUNION: Christ is the image of the invisible God. Here at this table, Christ has been revealed to us in bread and wine. Christ is the head of the body, the church. Here at this table, we have become one in Christ with believers throughout the world. May we go now in the name of Christ, bearing the good news of God's love through word and deed.

Proper 12
Sunday between July 24 and 30

Hosea 1:2–10
Psalm 85
Colossians 2:6–15 (16–19)
Luke 11:1–13

PRAYER FOR THE BREAD: God of light and life, you are the giver of all good gifts. You have given us the gift of life and the daily bread necessary to sustain it. You have given us the gift of prophets, who have helped us learn your way. And you have given us the gift of your son, Jesus Christ, who taught us that we could come to you in prayer, and who gave us this meal. As we come to break bread together, give us grateful and joyous hearts. By your Spirit, fill us with your love so that it overflows and reaches out to others. Amen.

PRAYER FOR THE CUP: We come to this table as a people who have received Jesus Christ as Lord, and as your children, parent God; teach us to receive Christ more fully. We come to this table as a people who struggle with forgiveness, merciful God; teach us to forgive ourselves, to forgive others, and to receive your forgiveness. We come to this table as a thirsty people, longing for your grace, gracious God. Bless this cup that we now lift, so that we may be satisfied. Help us be rooted in your Spirit, established in faith, and committed to your peace. Amen.

UNIFIED PRAYER: We remember the words of the psalmist: "Steadfast love and faithfulness will meet; righteousness and peace will kiss each other." Gracious God, we realize that this table is a sign of your steadfast love and faithfulness, a remembrance of the righteousness and peace of Jesus Christ. Here we eat the bread and remember that you feed your children and that Jesus Christ is the living bread. Here we drink the cup and remember Christ's love poured out for us. Bless us with your Spirit, so that our lives may radiate love and faithfulness, justice, and peace. Amen.

PRAYER AFTER COMMUNION: We have been buried with Christ in our baptism and have risen to new life, O living God. We have shared in this new life in Christ as we have dined at this table. Help our lives overflow with thanksgiving. Grant us your peace as we go from this place. Amen.

Proper 13
Sunday between July 31 and August 6

Hosea 11:1–11
Psalm 107:1–9, 43
Colossians 3:1–11
Luke 12:13–21

PRAYER FOR THE BREAD: Many treasures tempt us, O God our creator. We think that in them we can find value for ourselves. At this table, help us realize that your love is the only treasure that lasts, the only treasure that can give our lives true value. At this table, we eat a simple meal, a little piece of bread that paradoxically is all we need. In it we celebrate your feast, a feast of love, with our savior, Jesus Christ. Amen.

PRAYER FOR THE CUP: Forgiving and renewing God, so many things divide us from one another in this world, divide us into rich and poor, nation and nation, race and race, man and woman. Yet in Jesus Christ we have received new life and a love that brings us together. As we drink this cup, we come together as your children, affirming that Christ is all in all and we are united, one with another. May we be united by your Spirit. Amen.

UNIFIED PRAYER: Like a loving parent, nurturing God, you have watched us take our first tentative steps in faith. You have picked us up when we stumbled. You have held us to your cheek with tenderness and compassion when we were lost and alone. Yet still we would not give ourselves to you, or trust and love you as we ought. In Jesus Christ you sent the ultimate expression of your love. In eating from this loaf, we remember that you walked among us in human form. In drinking this cup, we remember that your love was poured out for us through Christ's death on the cross. May this time of communion remind us of the depths of your love and enable us to live as you would have us live. Bless us in your Spirit's presence. Amen.

PRAYER AFTER COMMUNION: We give you thanks, redeeming God, for your steadfast love endures forever. This table of communion symbolizes your love and helps us see your saving power in Jesus Christ. As we go from here, let your love shine through us that others may give you thanks. Amen.

Proper 14
Sunday between August 7 and 13

Isaiah 1:1, 10–20
Psalm 50:1–8, 22–23
Hebrews 11:1–3, 8–16
Luke 12:32–40

PRAYER FOR THE BREAD: God of Abraham and Sarah, Mary and Jesus, through the ages you have called your people to follow you on the paths of faith. When your people have called out in hunger, you have given them bread. Here at this table, we come in faith to receive the bread of life. As we eat this bread, help us remember the living Christ, who stayed true to you even in the shadow of the cross. Open our hearts to your Spirit so that we may grow in faith to you and in love and service to our neighbors. Amen.

PRAYER FOR THE CUP: Beneath the forms and movements of outward ritual, dear God, help us find inward meaning and purpose. Here at this table, help us remember the love of Christ that can transform our lives. May the cup we drink now be a symbol of our willingness to follow Christ in paths of service and commitment. Through your Spirit let your love work within us and shine through us. Amen.

UNIFIED PRAYER: Almighty God, help us remember that we have come to this table not to carry out an obligation, but to receive a gift. Raise our understanding of this moment so that we may realize the awesome love that has been poured out on us in Jesus Christ. Here we eat bread and drink wine in your presence in honor of a love that endured death so that we might live. As we do so, help us realize that as you have loved us, you call us to love others. As you have granted us mercy, you call us to be merciful. As you have fed us, you call us to feed a hungry world. Fill us with your Spirit that we may live in such a way that others may see your love in us. Amen.

PRAYER AFTER COMMUNION: At this table, you have shown us the right way, the way of salvation. Here we give our thanks. Help us go into the world and live our thanks. Amen.

Proper 15
Sunday between August 14 and 20

Isaiah 5:1−7
Psalm 80:1−2, 8−19
Hebrews 11:29−12:2
Luke 12:49−56

PRAYER FOR THE BREAD: Through the ages you have called your people to faith and trust, dear God. You have nurtured them and guided them. Today, as your people in this age and place, we come to be fed and nourished. In breaking and eating this bread, we acknowledge that you sent Jesus Christ to be the bread of life. Bless us as we bless this bread. As you feed us at this table, help us feed others, both physically and spiritually. May your Spirit guide us in the paths of peace. Amen.

PRAYER FOR THE CUP: You have planted seeds of faith in your children, O loving God. You have planted and cultivated, nurtured and tended us that we may grow in faith and love and that we may bear the fruit of mercy and compassion. In the wine we drink, we remember that we are called to be your vineyard, nourishing a thirsty world with the wine of Christ's love. Help us by your Spirit, we pray, to have a fruitful faith, a rooted love, for you and for all our brothers and sisters. Amen.

UNIFIED PRAYER: You are the God of the ages, our heritage and our hope. As we gather at this table, help us remember that we are not alone, but are part of a worldwide church that has existed through the ages. Help us be aware of the great cloud of witnesses, the saints of the ages, who have kept true to the faith. Help us remember as we eat this bread and drink this cup that we are part of Christ's family, part of the communion of saints. May their faith strengthen our faith, and may your Spirit nourish our spirits. Amen.

PRAYER AFTER COMMUNION: God of history and hope, we leave this table of communion knowing that we are never out of communion with you nor distant from our sisters and brothers in faith. Encourage us by your Spirit as we face the challenges of life. Amen.

Proper 16
Sunday between August 21 and 27

Jeremiah 1:4–10
Psalm 71:1–6
Hebrews 12:18–29
Luke 13:10–17

PRAYER FOR THE BREAD: We come to you in a spirit of reverence and awe, dear God, remembering your gift of Christ Jesus. Through Christ you have called us to a heavenly reign, one that cannot be shaken. As we eat the bread, we remember the Christ at the table with the disciples, and we praise the living Christ here with us today. Bless us in your Spirit. Amen.

PRAYER FOR THE CUP: Once we were aimless; now we are called. Once we were broken; now we have felt your healing touch. Once we were alone; now we are members of a covenant community. This cup is a sign of that calling, that healing, that community that we have been given in Christ Jesus. Bless us in your Spirit as we partake. Amen.

UNIFIED PRAYER: In the rush of our daily lives, we are so often distracted. We ignore your holiness, your power, and your love. In the quiet of these moments we come to be with you, to give you praise, to turn our hearts to you. As we share this bread and cup, we realize in deep humility and awe that you are with us. Speak to us in the silence; transform us with your love; lead us by your Spirit. Amen.

PRAYER AFTER COMMUNION: For peace, for silence, for the elements of communion that help us be aware of Christ's presence, we praise you, O God. As you have called us into your presence in this time, let us be aware of your presence with us in all times. Amen.

Proper 17
Sunday between August 28
and September 3

Jeremiah 2:4–13
Psalm 81:1, 10–16
Hebrews 13:1–8, 15–16
Luke 14:1, 7–14

PRAYER FOR THE BREAD: How often we stray from you, loving God, how often we ignore your invitations to partake of the fullness of life. We desperately scramble for that which does not satisfy and long for that which does not nourish. Still you patiently call us. You wish to feed us with the finest wheat, with honey from the rock. Help us hear and accept your invitation to feed us with the living bread, Jesus Christ, for in him we find life at its fullest. Help us find satisfaction in the love that Christ offers us here. When your Spirit calls us to follow, give us the grace to walk in your ways. Amen.

PRAYER FOR THE CUP: In this world, often we are judged or judge others by our money, looks, or power. At this table, compassionate God, we are judged by other standards. As we have received your hospitality, so you expect us to reach out in love to others. As we have received your forgiveness, so you expect us to forgive others. As we have received your grace, so you expect us to be loving and kind. May this cup we drink bring us closer in spirit to the Christ who has called us here. Amen.

UNIFIED PRAYER: You are the host who welcomes us to this table, gracious God. Here we are fed by your grace. It is your bread that we eat, your cup that we drink. Give us a humble spirit as we receive this gift. Give us a spirit of generosity, so that we may freely give to others who are hungry and thirsty, who are dispossessed and homeless, who are sick and outcast. Lead us beyond selfishness and arrogance to lives of humility and compassion. For we know that we can come to this table only because of the love of our humble and compassionate savior, Jesus Christ. Through your Spirit we come. Amen.

PRAYER AFTER COMMUNION: We have been in the presence of the living Christ, who is the same yesterday, today, and forever. We thank you, dear God, for the Christ who invited us here, the Christ who is with us always. Amen.

Proper 18
Sunday between September 4 and 10

Jeremiah 18:1–11
Psalm 139:1–6, 13–18
Philemon 1–21
Luke 14:25–33

PRAYER FOR THE BREAD: You have searched us and known us, dear God, better than we can ever know ourselves. Yet you still loved us enough to send us your son, Jesus Christ, that we might know your love and salvation. Help us realize as we eat this bread that we do not deserve to be here, but are here by your grace. May we remember here the love that Christ had for the disciples and the love that you have for all your children. And may we live out that love in each day, strengthened by your Spirit. Amen.

PRAYER FOR THE CUP: We are often slaves to our own desires and fears, redeeming God. But in Jesus Christ you have given us the freedom that casts out fears and have welcomed us into your family, not as slaves, but as brothers and sisters. Now as we gather at your family table, the cup we drink helps us remember that we were purchased at a price, that Christ's sacrifice made us free. Help us live in your freedom and bring freedom to others by your Spirit's power. Amen.

UNIFIED PRAYER:

"Have thine own way, Lord, have thine own way!
Thou art the potter, I am the clay.
Mold me and make me after thy will,
while I am waiting, yielded and still."*

We come to this table wanting to be your people, dear God, wanting you to form us after the fashion of Christ. We eat this bread, knowing that Christ is the living bread, and in him we find life. We drink from this cup, knowing that Christ poured out his life for us. Draw us closer to Christ in our eating and in our drinking, that we may live as you would have us live. In your Spirit's name we pray. Amen.

PRAYER AFTER COMMUNION: We have gathered here at this table in heightened awareness of your presence with us. Help us recall from these sacred moments that all the moments of our days are sacred, that wherever we go, you are with us. May we always be in communion with you through your Spirit. Amen.

---

*Adelaide A. Pollard, "Have Thine Own Way, Lord" (1902).

Proper 19
Sunday between September 11 and 17

Jeremiah 4:11–12, 22–28
Psalm 14
1 Timothy 1:12–17
Luke 15:1–10

PRAYER FOR THE BREAD: God of love, you have called us to love you, and we have loved things. God of mercy, you have called us to forgive others, and we have been spiteful and cold. God of peace, you have called us to be peacemakers, and we have been aggressive and intolerant. Yet this communion table is a sign to us that your love never gives up, that your mercy outweighs our selfishness, and that your peace can transform us and our broken relationships. In eating this bread, we who are so often weak find the strength we need to try again to live as you want us to live, following Jesus Christ. Help us remember through these moments of communion to follow your Spirit's call. Amen.

PRAYER FOR THE CUP: Gracious God, we have often been an ignorant and unbelieving people, seeking our own selfish ways. Even though we were undeserving, you came to us in Jesus Christ. Through Christ your grace overflowed, so that we might find faith and love. As we drink this cup, help us remember and accept this overflowing grace. Help us to be merciful, as we have received your mercy. Transform us by your Spirit's power. Amen.

UNIFIED PRAYER: Seeking God, you came for us when we were lost. You sought us out when we had strayed. In compassion and mercy, you led us back to you through Jesus Christ. All the heavens rejoice when your lost children come home. Here at this table, we feel at home; we feel the joy of being in your presence. The bread we eat and the cup we drink are symbols of your seeking love through Jesus Christ. In sharing them, we look forward to the heavenly feast to which you have called us. When we would wander, when we would become lost and confused, let your seeking Spirit find us and bring us home. Amen.

PRAYER AFTER COMMUNION: Immortal, invisible, only God, we have been in your presence in these holy moments of communion. To you be honor and glory forever and ever. Amen.

Proper 20
Sunday between September 18 and 24

Jeremiah 8:18—9:1
Psalm 79:1—9
1 Timothy 2:1—7
Luke 16:1—13

PRAYER FOR THE BREAD: Loving God, it is so often difficult for us to sort out means from ends, to value you and the people around us more than we value money, security, and power. We realize that this table is the place where we come to remember the price of our own salvation. Help us, as we break this bread, to care for you and for one another more than we care for all earthly treasures. Help us, as we eat this bread, to find in Christ our true master, the Lord of love. Sustain us by your Spirit's presence as we seek to be faithful to the way of Christ. Amen.

PRAYER FOR THE CUP: Compassionate God, you grieved for your people as we followed idols and lies. You called, and we did not listen. You offered health and peace, and we followed the paths of destruction. Through Jesus Christ, you came to save us and to bring us health and peace. As we drink this cup, we remember Christ's sacrifice, when your healing love was poured out as a balm for all of us. Help us to live by your Spirit, that we may help bring healing and love to this broken world. Amen.

UNIFIED PRAYER: We lift our prayers to you, saving God, and thank you for the new life we have received in Jesus Christ. We know that it is your desire to save all your children, so much so that you sent Jesus to show us your way, to ransom and redeem us. We gather at this table to celebrate this gift of salvation. Here we remember, as we break bread, the one who is the living bread. Here we remember, as we drink from the cup, the one whose life was poured out for all. Help us by the power of the Spirit to know the peace of the Spirit, through Jesus Christ, our Lord. Amen.

PRAYER AFTER COMMUNION: We are your people, dear God, the sheep of your pasture. At this table we have been fed and watered by your mighty hand. Our prayers of thanksgiving rise to you for these moments of communion and for all the times that we are led by your love. Amen.

Proper 21
Sunday between September 25 and October 1

Jeremiah 32:1–3a, 6–15
Psalm 91:1–6, 14–16
1 Timothy 6:6–19
Luke 16:19–31

PRAYER FOR THE BREAD: You are our refuge and our fortress, dear God. You watch over us and protect us. You care for our needs. Here at this table, where we break the bread that reminds us of our Savior's broken body, we remember that your love never gives up. As we eat this bread, we give you thanks for showing us salvation. We pray that the generosity of your Spirit may transform our spirits, that we too may care for, reach out to, and help those in need as you came to us in our need. Amen.

PRAYER FOR THE CUP: God of justice and mercy, we confess that we often think only of our own needs and desires and ignore those around us who are in poverty. Teach us to have compassionate hearts, that we might willingly help our neighbors in need. For it was in our need that you came to help us, through Jesus Christ. This cup is a reminder of Christ's compassion, of his willingness to give of himself that others might be saved. Bless us by your Spirit as we drink from it, that we may become more Christlike in our love. Amen.

UNIFIED PRAYER: We live each day in the shelter of your love, gracious God. You deliver us by your saving power from that which would destroy us. This very table at which we gather is a sign of your mercy and love. In this bread that we now eat, in this cup that we now drink, we affirm the mystery of your love and compassion. For you were once in our midst in human flesh and are still in our midst by the power of your Spirit. Bless us as we partake, so that the living Christ may work in us and through us. Amen.

PRAYER AFTER COMMUNION: Thank you for the opportunity to come to your table again, gracious God, and for the new life of the Spirit that we have received through Jesus Christ. May what we have experienced here help us pursue righteousness, godliness, faith, love, endurance, and gentleness in our daily lives. Amen.

Proper 22
Sunday between October 2 and 8

Lamentations 1:1–6
Lamentations 3:19–26 or Psalm 137
2 Timothy 1:1–14
Luke 17:5–10

PRAYER FOR THE BREAD: We have gathered at this table with thankful hearts, dear God. We are thankful for your church, for our brothers and sisters in faith, for all the ways you sustain and support our lives, and for daily bread. As we bless and eat this bread of communion, we thank you for the faith and the love we have received through Christ Jesus. We pray that the thankfulness we feel for this time of communion may transform our lives, filling them with joy and peace. As we have been fed, help us learn to feed others. Amen.

PRAYER FOR THE CUP: Forgiving God, we are a people of little faith. We are afraid to trust the power of your love. As such, our lives become fearful and selfish. Yet at this table, we are always given another chance. Here, as we pour the wine, we recall the Christ, the one who poured out his life in generosity and compassion. Through the power of your Spirit, help us learn by Christ's example to be self-giving, that we might serve you by loving our neighbors. Amen.

UNIFIED PRAYER: Great is your faithfulness, O God. Your steadfast love never ends; your mercy never ceases. Through the centuries you have blessed your people. Here at this, your table, we come in trust and hope. As we taste life in eating this bread and drinking this cup, we realize that Jesus Christ tasted death for us all. Make us more dedicated to your will, that we may follow the example of Christ. For it is he who lived out the message that to be great, we must serve and that to find life, we must be willing to lose it in Christ's service. Amen.

PRAYER AFTER COMMUNION: Gracious God, help us remember that we have been called to this table not by our own goodness but by your saving grace. As we have relied on your mercy here, help us to be aware of your mercy and grace during all our days and hours. Give us grateful hearts and spirits tuned to your Spirit. Amen.

Proper 23
Sunday between October 9 and 15

Jeremiah 29:1, 4–7
Psalm 66:1–12
2 Timothy 2:8–15
Luke 17:11–19

PRAYER FOR THE BREAD: When we are lost and confused, O wise God, you give us direction. When we are hopeless and desolate, encouraging God, you give us hope. When we are weak and hungry, compassionate God, you give us bread. We come here to this table rejoicing that we have been given the bread of life in Jesus Christ. Bless us by your Spirit as we partake in Christ's name. Amen.

PRAYER FOR THE CUP: Loving God, we come to you in need of healing, of wholeness, of forgiveness. Help us trust your love for us, that we may have the courage to ask for your healing touch. As we drink this cup, let it bring the peace of the Spirit to our lives. And give us the faith to be truly thankful for all that we have received through Jesus Christ, our savior. Amen.

UNIFIED PRAYER: We come here, dear God, to remember Jesus Christ, who faced death for us, and who was raised from the dead. In Christ, we experience the good news of your love for all humankind. Help us remember, as we eat the bread, that Christ's body was given for us. Help us remember, as we drink the cup, the blood of the new covenant, spilled for the forgiveness of sins. May this meal be for us not only a time of remembrance but also a time of hope, a time to anticipate the eternal communion we will share in your presence. Amen.

STATEMENT AFTER COMMUNION: Bless our God, O peoples, let the sound of God's praise be heard. We thank our God for giving us Jesus Christ, whose presence we celebrated at this table today.

Proper 24
Sunday between October 16 and 22

Jeremiah 31:27–34
Psalm 119:97–104
2 Timothy 3:14–4:5
Luke 18:1–8

PRAYER FOR THE BREAD: God of grace and power, we your children come to be fed. Often we ignore your ways and violate your word, living selfish and fearful lives. Yet still you call us, still you seek us, still you welcome us. We see this table, this bread, as a reminder of your steadfast love given us through Jesus Christ. As we eat this bread, we remember Christ's love for the disciples, and we celebrate Christ's love for us. Through your Spirit, may we grow in love for one another. Amen.

PRAYER FOR THE CUP: We are called to covenant by your voice, redeemer God. We are called to covenant by the faithful people and prophets down through the ages. We are called in covenant as part of your church. Most of all, we are called in covenant by Jesus Christ our Lord, who offered his life for us. As we drink this cup, we remember that Christ, whose blood was shed for us, sealed the covenant. Help us through your Spirit to live justly and lovingly, faithful to the covenant we have received. Amen.

UNIFIED PRAYER: In your son, Jesus Christ, we have received a new covenant. In your son, Jesus Christ, your word has been written upon our hearts. As we come to this table, we praise you and we praise Jesus for the love that alone can bring us to faith in you. As we eat the bread, we remember Christ's body given for us. As we drink the cup, we remember that the new covenant was sealed at the cost of our savior's life. Help us now be Spirit-led, so that the new covenant written in our hearts may also be written in our words and deeds. As you seek justice for all your children, teach us to reach out and help bring your ways to an unjust world. Amen.

PRAYER AFTER COMMUNION: We love your words, dear God, for they show us the ways of love. We love coming to your table, where we find your love shining through this sacred meal. Bless us by your Spirit as we leave this place, and help us taste your goodness in each hour of every day. Amen.

Proper 25
Sunday between October 23 and 29

Joel 2:23–32
Psalm 65
2 Timothy 4:6–8, 16–18
Luke 18:9–14

PRAYER FOR THE BREAD: What a wonderful creation you have made, generous God. The skies bring rain that supports life. The grain on the hillside shouts for joy. Out of that grain, we make bread to bring us joy and to nourish our bodies. Here at your table, we take that bread and bless it and remember that you sent Jesus Christ as the living bread. Bless us as we partake; keep us sensitive to the presence of your Spirit. Help stir within us the desire to share the good things of your creation with others, as you have done for us. Amen.

PRAYER FOR THE CUP: You have poured out your love for your people, self-giving God. We have been blessed with your love even as we have been blessed with life. You sent us Jesus Christ, who poured out his life for our sakes that we might realize the fullness of your love. Inspired by him, apostles and martyrs, pastors and teachers, missionaries and parents have given of themselves that others might know Christ's love. Bless us by your Spirit as we drink this cup so that we may always remember your self-giving love and so that we may learn to love as we have been loved. Amen.

UNIFIED PRAYER: By awesome deeds you have saved your people, mighty God. Through the centuries you have raised the lowly, freed the slaves, and liberated the oppressed. You have inspired your children with dreams and visions of a world united in your love. As we come to this table of communion, we pray that you will give us humble spirits, so that we realize that we are here not because of our own goodness, but because of yours. We have taken the grain and the grapes that you have given us and made them into bread and wine. Now we offer it up to you, so that through it we might realize the presence of the living Christ. It is this Christ who said, "Take, eat, this is my body"; and "Take, drink, this is my blood." We partake at Christ's invitation. By your Spirit's presence and power, unite our hearts in love for you, for one another, and for a needy world. Amen.

PRAYER AFTER COMMUNION: Praise is due you, O God. You answer your people's prayers. You have given us this time of communion to bring us together in Christ's presence. We thank you for having been to your table. Help us by your Spirit to live Christ-centered lives. Amen.

Proper 26
Sunday between October 30
and November 5

Habakkuk 1:1–4; 2:1–4
Psalm 119:137–144
2 Thessalonians 1:1–4, 11–12
Luke 19:1–10

PRAYER FOR THE BREAD: We come to Christ's table, dear God, surprised that we have been invited. We know we are not worthy, yet here we find your acceptance. In taking this bread, blessing it, breaking it, and eating, we remember the Christ who came to give us new life. Through Christ, you have called us to be children of Abraham, your children. Help us grow in our faith and love as we seek to follow our savior. Amen.

PRAYER FOR THE CUP: Loving and just God, we come as sinners needing forgiveness; we come as self-righteous people needing humility; we come as anxious people needing your peace. Because of your love for human-kind, you sent Jesus Christ to set us free from selfishness and sin. Here at this table, we reaffirm our faith in Christ and rejoice in his presence. Bless us by your Spirit as we drink from this cup, for we have your promise that Christ's overflowing love will give us overflowing life. Amen.

UNIFIED PRAYER: You are righteous, O God, not with a righteousness that condemns, but with a righteousness that redeems. You have given us law so that we may know your way, and you have given us grace so that when we stray, you are there to forgive us and give us a new beginning. We are tempted by the standards of the world, dear God, to follow values that are based on injustice and greed. Yet we know that you still invite us to dine with you. As we eat this bread and drink from this cup, help our hearts overflow with joy at having received Christ into our lives. Through your Spirit, teach us your generosity and your passion for justice. Help us learn at this table that true joy in life lies not in taking, but in giving. Amen.

PRAYER AFTER COMMUNION: We have come to this table so that Jesus Christ's name may be glorified, according to your grace, O God. Thank you for bidding us come. May your Spirit guide us on the paths of peace and love as we go. Amen.

Proper 27
Sunday between November 6 and 12

Haggai 1:15b–2:9
Psalm 145:1–5, 17–21 or Psalm 98
2 Thessalonians 2:1–5, 13–17
Luke 20:27–38

PRAYER FOR THE BREAD: God of light and life, we come to you as a people who are often complacent and comfortable with living in the shadows, plodding through dull routines. Even coming to this table can seem like a routine if we don't pay attention to its true meaning. Yet you have done something new here, something powerful and transforming. You have given yourself in love through Jesus Christ, and now you offer us the light and life of the living Christ, the one who conquered death. Awaken us to the power of Christ as we eat this bread, and help us lift to you a new song, a song of victory and joy. Through your Spirit we pray. Amen.

PRAYER FOR THE CUP: All creation witnesses to your glory, O God of the ages. The seas roar, and the hills sing together for joy at your presence. All history is in your hand; time and eternity are your creations. Yet you have come to us in Jesus Christ, gently and humbly, that we might realize your love and accept the life you offer. The cup we raise now helps us to remember the Christ who died, helps us to be aware of the Christ who lives now and helps us to have hope in the Christ who will come again. Grant us your Spirit as we drink from the cup that Christ has set before us, that our lives may reflect your glory. Amen.

UNIFIED PRAYER: Every day we bless you, dear God, and praise your name forever. Your ways are wondrous, your splendor glorious. And yet in all your glory you are near to us. You watch over all your children with care and compassion. This communion table stands to us as a sign of a love that never fails. At it we remember Jesus Christ, who came to show us your love. The bread we eat, the cup we drink are signs of Christ's sacrifice, of Christ's victory over death, and of Christ's presence with us. Fill our hearts with the love of Christ that we might serve and love others. Amen.

PRAYER AFTER COMMUNION: From generation to generation your people have gathered around this table, gracious God, to meet the living Christ. We thank you for having come here today. Help us each and all to witness to the light and love that we have experienced here. Amen.

Proper 28
Sunday between November 13 and 19

Isaiah 65:17–25
Isaiah 12
2 Thessalonians 3:6–13
Luke 21:5–19

PRAYER FOR THE BREAD: We bring bread to this table, the work of human hands, of bakers and millers, farmers and truckers. Yet we know this bread is made from wheat, part of the great gift of life you have given us. Bless us as we gather at your table to eat this bread, and bless all who have helped shape it, bake it, and bring it here. This bread is a small part of the food that sustains us physically, dear God, yet it is a large part of what sustains us spiritually. In it we receive a blessing as we realize that Christ is truly with us. As we share the bread now, give us generous hearts and committed hands that we may feed others physically and spiritually, even as we have been fed. Amen.

PRAYER FOR THE CUP: You are a God who makes things new. When we are tired and discouraged, lazy and apathetic, you challenge us to new life, to new hope, to new work. In the death of Christ you have taken the cross, a symbol of hatred and evil, and transformed it into a sign of love and hope. We come now to drink this cup together, remembering that Christ's blood was shed for a new covenant, a new beginning in the relationship between you and humankind. Let us find in it new life in your Spirit, so that we may witness to your love through our daily lives. Amen.

UNIFIED PRAYER: You are the living God, the God of Abraham and Sarah, Isaac and Rebekah, Jacob and Rachel; the God of Moses and the prophets; the God of Jesus Christ and the disciples. In you we have our life. Here at this table we come to celebrate the Lord's supper and to proclaim the presence of the living Christ in our midst. As we eat this bread, we remember that Christ is the living bread. As we drink this cup, we celebrate that Christ is the living water who sustains and refreshes us all. Bless us by your Spirit, so that we may be inspired to serve you in our daily lives. Amen.

PRAYER AFTER COMMUNION: With joy we have drawn water from the wells of salvation. The bread we ate and the wine we drank were for us signs of the presence of the risen Christ in our midst. We sing your praises, great and loving God, for having given us the opportunity to commune together today. Amen.

Proper 29
Sunday between November 20 and 26
(Reign of Christ Sunday)

Jeremiah 23:1–6
Luke 1:68–79
Colossians 1:11–20
Luke 23:33–43

PRAYER FOR THE BREAD: There are many who would seek to lead us, O God, many who want to persuade us that their ideology or product or group is best. Help us hold fast to you, to your will and your way, as expressed through Jesus the Christ. Help us remember that through Jesus Christ, you are the good shepherd. As we eat this bread of communion, help us remember that Christ gave his life so that we might have life. Strengthen us by your Spirit so that we may hold fast to Christ. Amen.

PRAYER FOR THE CUP: We bless you, loving God, for you have remembered your people in their need. You have raised up a mighty savior, Jesus Christ, so that we might know the power of your salvation. As we drink this cup, we remember Christ, who sealed the new covenant with his blood. Here we taste your love; here our feet are guided upon the paths of your peace. Through your Spirit, help us know the power of your forgiveness, so that we might forgive others. Amen.

UNIFIED PRAYER: Through Jesus Christ, dear God, we have been given the power of thankful, transformed lives. We have been rescued from that which would destroy us and been given an inheritance as saints. At the table that is now set before us, we recall Christ's sacrifice, we celebrate Christ's power over death, and we give thanks for Christ's tender mercies in our lives. Bless this bread, which helps us recall that all things created point to the work of Christ. Bless this cup, which reminds us that you reconciled us to yourself by making peace through the blood of the cross. Through your Spirit, help us live reconciled, reconciling lives. Amen.

STATEMENT AFTER COMMUNION: Jesus Christ reigns! Even though sin, violence, and oppression abound, God's grace through Jesus Christ abounds even more. The dawn has broken, and we can walk in the light. Let us go from this table a redeemed people, a people who know their savior's love. Let us go from this table a healing people, a forgiving people, a transformed people, whose very lives echo the statement "Jesus Christ reigns."

Scripture Index

1:68–79	Advent 2, Proper 29
2:(1–7) 8–20	Christmas Eve/Christmas Day
2:1–14 (15–20)	Christmas Eve/Christmas Day
2:41–52	Christmas 1
3:1–6	Advent 2
3:7–18	Advent 3
3:15–17, 21–22	Epiphany 1
4:1–13	Lent 1
4:14–21	Epiphany 3
4:21–30	Epiphany 4
5:1–11	Epiphany 5
6:17–26	Epiphany 6
6:27–38	Epiphany 7
6:39–49	Epiphany 8
7:1–10	Proper 4
7:11–17	Proper 5
7:36–8:3	Proper 6
8:26–39	Proper 7
9:28–36	Lent 2
9:28–36 (37–43)	Last Sunday after Epiphany
9:51–62	Proper 8
10:1–11, 16–20	Proper 9
10:25–37	Proper 10
10:38–42	Proper 11
11:1–13	Proper 12
12:13–21	Proper 13
12:32–40	Proper 14
12:49–56	Proper 15
13:1–9	Lent 3
13:10–17	Proper 16
13:31–35	Lent 2
14:1, 7–14	Proper 17
14:25–33	Proper 18
15:1–3, 11b–32	Lent 4
15:1–10	Proper 19

9:1–6 (7–20)	Easter 3
9:36–43	Easter 4
10:34–43	Easter Day
11:1–6	Easter 5
16:9–15	Easter 6
16:16–34	Easter 7

Romans

5:1–5	Trinity Sunday
8:14–17	Pentecost
10:8b–13	Lent 1

1 Corinthians

10:1–13	Lent 3
11:23–36	Maundy Thursday
12:1–11	Epiphany 2
12:12–31a	Epiphany 3
13:1–13	Epiphany 4
15:1–11	Epiphany 5
15:12–20	Epiphany 6
15:19–26	Easter Day
15:35–38, 42–50	Epiphany 7
15:51–58	Epiphany 8

2 Corinthians

3:12–4:2	Last Sunday after Epiphany
5:16–21	Lent 4

Galatians

1:1–12	Proper 4
1:11–24	Proper 5
2:15–21	Proper 6
3:23–29	Proper 7
5:1, 13–25	Proper 8
6:(1–6) 7–16	Proper 9

Ephesians

1:3–14	Christmas 2
3:1–12	Epiphany

Hebrews

1:1–4 (5–12)	Christmas Eve/Christmas Day
10:5–10	Advent 4
11:1–3, 8–16	Proper 14
11:29–12:2	Proper 15
12:18–29	Proper 16
13:1–8, 15–16	Proper 17

Revelation

1:4–8	Easter 2
5:11–14	Easter 3
7:9–17	Easter 4
21:1–6	Easter 5
21:1–10, 21:22–22:5	Easter 6
22:12–14, 16–17, 20–21	Easter 7